SPOTLIGHT ON
SPECIAL EDUCATIONAL NEEDS:

SPECIFIC LEARNING DIFFICULTIES

DOROTHY SMITH

A NASEN Publication

Published in 1996
Second Edition 2003

ISBN 0 906730 89 9

Published by NASEN.
NASEN is a registered charity. Charity No. 1007023.
NASEN is a company limited by guarantee, registered in England and Wales.
Company No. 2637438.

Further copies of this book and details of NASEN's many other publications
may be obtained from the NASEN Bookshop at its registered office:
NASEN House, 4/5 Amber Business Village, Amber Close, Amington,
Tamworth, Staffs. B77 4RP.
Tel: 01827 311500; Fax: 01827 313005; Email: welcome@nasen.org.uk
Website: www.nasen.org.uk

Copy editing by Nicola von Schreiber.
Cover design by Mark Procter.
Typeset in Times by J. C. Typesetting and printed in the United Kingdom
by Stowes, Stoke-on-Trent.

SPOTLIGHT ON SPECIAL EDUCATIONAL NEEDS: SPECIFIC LEARNING DIFFICULTIES

Contents

Acknowledgements

The author and publishers wish to express their grateful thanks to Alec Williams and Mike Hinson for their helpful suggestions and comments on the original version of this book.

The extract from the *Individual Reading Analysis* © by Denis Vincent and Michael de la Mare, 1989, 1992 on page 41; the extract from the *New Reading Analysis* © by Denis Vincent and Michael de la Mare, 1985 on page 42; the extract from the *Graded Word Reading List* © NFER-Nelson 1992 on page 44 are all reproduced with the permission of the publishers NFER-Nelson, Darville House, 2 Oxford Road East, Windsor SL4 1DF.

Please note that all children's names in the examples quoted have been changed to preserve their anonymity. When parents are mentioned this also refers to 'carers'.

SPOTLIGHT ON SPECIAL EDUCATIONAL NEEDS: SPECIFIC LEARNING DIFFICULTIES

Introduction

'Some children may have significant difficulties in reading, writing, spelling or manipulating number, which are not typical of their general level of performance. They may gain some skills in some subjects quickly and demonstrate a high level of ability orally, yet may encounter sustained difficulty in gaining literacy or numeracy skills. Such children can become severely frustrated and may also have emotional and/or behavioural difficulties.'

(DfEE, 1994, para. 3:60)

Where the new *Special Educational Needs Code of Practice* (DfES, 2001) is concerned the term 'specific learning difficulties' is not given a definition but is mentioned within two of the four broad categories of special educational needs (SEN). It is a subdivision of cognition and learning, the other learning difficulties being moderate, severe or profound, whereas previously it was a category in its own right. Like the *Code of Practice on the Identification and Assessment of Special Educational Needs* (1994) this Code mentions the word 'dyslexia' as an example of a specific learning difficulty. This can be noted as follows under the heading 'cognition and learning':

'Children who demonstrate features of ... specific learning difficulties, such as dyslexia or dyspraxia, require specific programmes to aid progress in cognition and learning.'

(*SEN Code of Practice*, DfES 2001, 7 para. 7:58)

However, specific learning difficulties is also mentioned under the heading of 'communication and interaction'. Again dyslexia and dyspraxia are given as examples. The Code of Practice (2001) recognises the uniqueness of individual children and that often their needs are interrelated and do not necessarily fit into any one category. Those who work within the field of specific learning difficulties are well aware of this fact.

The main thrust of this publication will be specific learning difficulties in its widest sense although there will be mention of some of the other often-used labels within this overarching category.

History

This distinction between a general learning difficulty and a specific learning difficulty has taken many years to be generated. Although it was recognised by some educators that there were individuals whose attainments in reading did not appear to match their probable intellectual levels and whose literacy problems were difficult to help, there were others who dismissed these suppositions. In fact the phrase 'word-blind' was coined as far back as 1877 and from this the dyslexia movement was born. However, official educational recognition of what now is termed 'specific learning difficulties' only appeared with the publication of *The Warnock Report* in 1978 (although dyslexia was recognised under the Chronically Sick and Disabled Persons Act of 1970).

Thus, within the past hundred years much has been achieved by individuals and organisations in order to gain recognition for adults and young people who have been assigned as 'dyslexic' or who now have been given the label as having 'specific learning difficulties'. Over the years the emphasis on the problem being solely one of reading difficulties has changed to encapsulate other factors, in particular the written word via spelling problems. The Code of Practice (2001) offers a broader picture, particularly as specific learning difficulties is no longer a separate category of needs and, therefore, in this publication some prominence will be given to a range of problems that pupils with specific learning difficulties may experience which include memory, literacy, sequencing and organisational skills, motor competencies and language areas.

Definition

One of the resulting difficulties over the years was that of an acceptable definition. These changed as educators tried to bring into a short statement the many problems that may be discovered in an individual with such difficulties. For example:

> *'Children with specific learning difficulties are those who, in the absence of sensory defect or overt organic damage, have an intractable learning problem in one of more of reading, writing, spelling and mathematics, and who do not respond to normal teaching.'*
> (Tansley & Pankhurst, 1981)

The above definition does not fully explain the underlying problems and features of those specific difficulties that are deeply established in certain individuals. Up to 10% of children have some specific problems and about 4% will be severely affected according to the British Dyslexia Association (*The Dyslexia Handbook*, 1995). The following interpretation may be more acceptable as it includes some of the other factors that may be present. This version is a compilation from varying sources. Specific learning difficulties are significant problems of:

- synthesising (bringing together information within the brain);

- organisation (making sense and order of this information);

- working memory (holding onto this information in order to use it at will).

These severe problems which restrict the individual's proficiencies in information processing produce an intractable (or hard to shift) learning problem in some or all of the skills of:

- reading;

- spelling;

- written work;

- numeracy;

which does not respond to normal classroom teaching. If unrecognised there may be instances of secondary emotional/behavioural problems.

Invariably it is the individual's *working memory*, both visual and auditory, (although for some, the problem may rest with only one of these) that is the key problem. The working memory is that part of the memory function which has to hold on to input collected from the senses (either immediate or brought back from long-term memory). This input or information has to be understood and organised (usually in some kind of sequence) before being applied and acted upon in some form and then returned to the long-term memory store. Therefore, if the working memory is weak then any process that demands its use (such as reading, spelling, numeracy, self-organisation) will be impaired.

Pupils with specific learning difficulties can come from any socio-cultural background and their intelligence can be measured at any level. This makes it a slight problem for some parents/carers and educators to understand the distinction between a general and a specific difficulty. What has to be

7

remembered is that a general learning difficulty is where a pupil finds learning and acquiring skills a problem in every area of the curriculum. This special educational need is dealt with fully in *Learning Difficulties* by Sally Beveridge (one of the books in NASEN's *Spotlight on Special Eductional Needs* series).

It is also important to remember that if a child has a problem that is *easily* dealt with and if it is one that *can* be helped within the resources of normal classroom teaching then by definition it cannot be severe or significant. And if it is not severe or significant it is not a serious specific learning difficulty. However, as with all problems there is a continuum of need and teachers need to be aware of all aspects of specific learning difficulties, from mild to moderate to severe.

It is not the intention of this book to discuss why specific learning difficulties occur, either genetically or neurologically. The References and Further Reading section will guide the reader towards such publications. There will be mention of the subsets of specific learning difficulties as indicated in the Code of Practice which could include areas such as dyslexia, dyspraxia, dyscalculia, dysgraphia and dysphasia. (Reference is made to these in the appendices as it is to scotopic sensitivity syndrome and ADD, attention deficit disorder.)

Attached to the Draft Code (DfEE, July 2000) which was a consultation paper was *SEN Thresholds: Good Practice Guidance on Identification and Provision for Pupils with Special Educational Needs.* In this there was set out a collection of factors which might be present in a pupil who is described as having specific learning difficulties. These covered the following:

- problems with gross and fine motor skills;

- low attainment in one or more curriculum areas in particular if this can be an indication of difficulties in literacy and/or numeracy skills;

- evidence that the learning difficulties are not global where certain areas of the curriculum show higher attainment than others;

- signs of frustration and/or low self-esteem which may be shown in behavioural problems;

- particular difficulties in areas such as sequencing, organisation, phonology and short-term memory;

8

- language difficulties particularly where younger children are concerned;

- difficulties and delays in forming concepts.

Although these are omitted from the Code of Practice (2001) they indicate the problems that can arise when recording the particular areas of need when using the label 'specific learning difficulties'.

This Spotlight book is intended to be a practical handbook, giving advice and helpful suggestions for class and subject teachers, with added ideas for parents/carers, based on the Code of Practice (2001). Where appropriate there will also be reference to the *SEN Toolkit* (DfES, 2001). Areas covered will be working in partnership with parents/carers; pupil participation; identification, assessment and provision in early education settings; the primary phase and the secondary sector; and the issues concerning statutory assessment and Statements. Because the Code contains general information about specific learning difficulties and pupils' particular learning needs, suggestions will be added from other sources.

The choice of a correct label can be important for the child. Some cope well with the term 'dyslexia' but others hate the thought of appearing different from their peers. The term 'learning difference' is becoming accepted as an educational term and this can be explained to the child in a more positive manner. The child is not lazy or unintelligent and there are areas in which he or she can cope in the same way as everyone else but also there are areas of difficulty, areas of difference. To help these latter areas means hard work but there are always ways to ease the problems or to find strategies of coping with them. Any labels needs to be associated with explanations and these should be given in as positive a manner as possible.

Identification

A great deal of work has gone into identifying what factors make up the profile of an individual with specific learning difficulties and researchers and other educators have identified various problems which can be present.

It is accepted that there is a continuum of problems where specific learning difficulties are concerned from mild to severe and that as individuals are not alike their own particular problems need not be exactly similar to those of others. Because of the varied nature of specific learning difficulties and the way that young people learn their basic skills some children's problems do not become apparent until the end of their primary or beginning of their secondary years. For some individuals specific learning difficulties are not suspected until examination work is started during further education. However, there are also those children who are thought to have specific learning difficulties before they start their school life, in the early years or Foundation Stage when children are within pre-school settings.

This conception of levels of difficulty is part of the new Code's message. Pupils with special educational needs may have either lower levels of difficulty or higher levels of difficulty depending on measured criteria and this determines the support allocated from within the early education setting, school or from the LEA. The terms used within the Code which indicate a change in interventions are 'School Action' and 'School Action Plus'. These terms will be discussed later.

It must be remembered whenever a child's performance is matched against any list of components that may indicate a specific problem that one must not leap to conclusions. Checklists or performance indicators only form part of the identification process. Also in most cases there would have to be a cluster of problems which would be the trigger for later closer assessment. Observations of children's learning behaviours in both the class and the home often can alert parents/carers and teachers to a problem in learning. These then can be explored in more detail and can be given attention. As will be stated later it is also important to determine what the child *can* do as well as examining the areas of difficulty. The Code uses the term 'graduated response' which stresses the fact that through careful monitoring it can be noted whether progress is, or is not, being satisfactorily made, either in general or specific terms. Intervention can then take place. What is suggested is that if progress is not as is expected then action that is additional or different should be set into motion.

Early identification

The *Code of Practice on the Identification and Assessment of Special Educational Needs* (DfEE, 1994) stated:

> *'Because early identification should lead to a more timely assessment and intervention which in turn should avoid the escalation of a difficulty into a significant special educational need, it is important that any concern about a child's development and progress should be shared at the earliest possible moment.'*

(para. 5:16)

10

The revised, new Code continues with this proposition and states:

'The importance of early identification, assessment and provision for any child who may have special educational needs cannot be over-emphasised. The earlier action is taken, the more responsive the child is likely to be, and the more readily can intervention be made without undue disruption to the organisation of the school. Assessment should not be regarded as a single event but rather as a continuing process.'

(para. 5.11)

'Identification, Assessment and Provision in Early Education Settings' is the title of Chapter 4 and 'Identification, Assessment and Provision in the Primary Phase' is dealt with in Chapter 5. In general terms identification and assessment should be ongoing and criteria such as the Early Learning Goals, baseline assessment and progress matched against the objectives set out in the National Literacy and Numeracy Strategy Frameworks are suggested for use. The publication *Curriculum Guidance for the Foundation Stage* (QCA/DfEE, 2000) is given as a reference.

There are certain checklists provided for parents/carers and professionals who work with pre-school and early years children which give indicators that could point to later specific learning difficulty problems (see the lists of positive criteria in this chapter). What has to be remembered is that however helpful these indicators can seem they are made up from some of the factors that can be found in the general course of learning in most children. Teachers have to be aware of when an apparent weakness might be developmental and routine and when it might cause concern. What appears to be far more important is to make sure that *all* pre-school children in early education settings, nurseries and playgroups and early years children in their reception school classes develop the mastery of certain 'early learning' skills if they are going to be able to learn to read and write successfully and to cope with later school life. These areas are:

- visual perception (what the pupil actually sees on the page and elsewhere); visual discrimination (how the pupil is able to see differences between words, letters and numbers); visual sequencing (the ability to perceive letters and words in the correct order); visual categorisation (knowledge of visual similarities between words and letters); and visual memory;

11

- auditory perception (the pupil's ability to hear sounds); auditory discrimination (how the pupil is able to hear differences in sounds); auditory sequencing (the ability to hear letters and words in the correct order); auditory categorisation (knowledge of similarities between the sounds of words and letters); and auditory memory;

- visual motor processing (the ability to produce, usually in writing, what is seen) and fine motor control;

- early number concepts;

- early phonological awareness (e.g. rhymes and alliteration);

- expressive and receptive language knowledge and usage adequate for early learning;

- ability to understand, process (internalise and make sense of) and carry out spoken instructions;

- ability to organise and process (internalise and make sense of) thoughts in order to express needs.

If a child finds problems with any of these broad indicators then early teaching programmes can be set up because these skills form the basis of later more 'formal' learning. There are references to books later in the References and Further Reading that give more detailed information about acquiring these necessary skills. Young children can be more easily identified as having potential learning problems if they show an uneven developmental profile where there are particular strengths and particular weaknesses.

It is possible to encounter problems when very early identification practices are set up. However, it can be likely that this 'labelling' could lead to lower or negative expectations being set in motion by those who come in contact with the young child. Also incorrect labelling may occur because the child might just be slower in developing the relevant skills. But it is generally felt that early identification, if handled correctly and sensitively, can be more beneficial than disadvantageous. More precise identification can lead to better targeted teaching because of the detailed description gained of the pupil's strengths and weaknesses.

Identification in the primary sector: early stages

The Code of Practice (2001) emphasises the helpfulness of the National Curriculum as an identification and monitoring tool. It states:

> *'All children in the primary sector should have access to the National Literacy and Numeracy Strategies alongside the National Curriculum. All schools will through their cycle of observation, assessment, planning and review make provision for increased curriculum differentiation, curricular adaptations, and pastoral or disciplinary procedures dependent on the individual child's strengths and weaknesses. A variety of approaches should be employed to maximise the achievement of all pupils.'*
>
> (para. 5.17)

As has already been mentioned there are checklists that purport to determine if a child has a specific or dyslexic learning difficulty and these can be damaging if used indiscriminately and without care. Some of the indicators are found in children's general learning and, therefore, teachers should be concerned only if problems persist for longer than is realistically expected. However, such lists could be used as a starting point especially if several of the points are found within the child's development. Put into broad categories the following could be used:

Language areas

- history of delayed speech and language development;

- difficulty with pronouncing multi-syllabic words;

- difficulty with sequencing and ordering in speech and language;

- difficulty in word labelling retrieval (being able to remember a particular word in speech).

Visual problems
Discrimination and sequencing:

- letter order confusion when reading;

- poor left-right discrimination;

- leaves letters out of words – puts letters in the wrong order;

13

- confusion of similar-looking letters;

- reversals of letters and figures;

- use of mirror writing.

Memory

- strange spelling patterns;

- difficulty in telling left from right;

- misreads core vocabulary.

Auditory problems
Discrimination and sequencing:

- difficulty with sound blending;

- difficulty with phonological awareness (rhyming words, alliteration) and syllable beating and segmentation (understanding how words are divided into syllables or parts);

- confusion of similar-sounding letters.

Memory

- difficulty in remembering the order of the days of the week, months of the year, the alphabet.

General

- early clumsiness;

- poor concentration span;

- similar familial history;

- lacks self-confidence;

- has 'good' and 'bad' days.

An example of how to use the above indicators to make an initial identification
Jake is 6 years old and because of his good understanding of language and oral ability and because he can cope with all areas of the National Curriculum except for reading and recording his class teacher and parents queried specific learning difficulties. The following indicators were noted with information being given by his parents and his teacher:

Language areas

- history of delayed speech and language development : no evidence

- difficulty with pronouncing multi-syllabic words : no problems

- difficulty with sequencing and ordering in speech and language : no problems

- difficulty in word labelling retrieval : no problems

Visual problems
Discrimination and sequencing:

- letter order confusion when reading : probable problems ('on/now')

- poor left-right discrimination : probable problems

- leaves letters out of words – puts letters in the wrong order : problems with copying

- confusion of similar-looking letters : problems with matching and recognising letters printed in different fonts

- reversals of letters and figures : 'b/d' confusion and some letters incorrectly oriented

- use of mirror writing : not seen

Memory

- strange spelling patterns   : as yet cannot spell

- difficulty in telling left from right   : yes

- misreads core vocabulary   : some problems seen

Auditory problems
Discrimination and sequencing:

- difficulty with sound blending   : couldn't cope from
                                        whispered sounds/didn't
                                        understand concepts
                                        of sameness and
                                        difference

- difficulty with phonological   : understands the concept
  awareness (rhyming words,   of rhyme and can
  alliteration) and syllable beating   syllable beat – can 'hear'
  and segmentation   and produce first sounds
                                        but not end sounds,
                                        seems to understand the
                                        concept of alliteration
                                        and has begun to read
                                        words with units of
                                        sounds, knows many
                                        letter sounds for saying
                                        and writing

- confusion of similar-sounding letters : 'd/t' confusion and 'e/i'
                                        when writing

Memory

- difficulty in remembering the order : problems here and has to
  of the days of the week, months of   use letter names as a prop
  the year, the alphabet   when spelling

16

General

- early clumsiness : no

- poor concentration span : yes

- similar familial history : father had spelling
problems as a boy

- lacks self-confidence : where reading is
concerned

- has 'good' and 'bad' days : no

There are some indications that Jake may have some specific learning difficulties and so his progress will be closely monitored. Particular emphasis will be given to visual discrimination activities, oral work on sounds and games for core word learning. Shared reading will be carried out because of his antagonism for this activity and his parents will be given games to reinforce the in-school teaching. His parents were pleased that Jake's early language skills caused no problems.

Identification in the primary sector: later stages

As a child grows older and is seen to be failing at the basic skills of reading and spelling although coping orally and in the more practical areas it is rather more easy to observe those 'performance indicators' which could indicate the specificity of the problem. These can be observed when the child is responding to classroom activities and are where:

- Performance in literacy skills is at a lower level than could be expected from performance in other curriculum areas.

- Performance is often inconsistent varying from day to day.

- Performance is varied dependent upon the child's mood (however, it should be noted that this is not expressly a specific problem).

- Oral language is often at a higher level than written language.

17

- Reading is slow and lacking in fluency.

- There are problems with phonic decoding and synthesis when reading.

- There are problems with remembering core keywords both in reading and spelling.

- Memory problems show themselves both with factual retention and more global recall.

- Spelling is bizarre and, therefore, uncommunicable.

- Words attempted for spelling contain incorrect letters and letter combinations for particular sounds.

- Spelling is inconsistent with previously learnt words spelt both correctly and incorrectly in one piece of writing.

- There are problems with pronouncing multi-syllabic words.

- Emotional/behavioural behaviours become evident because of lack of self-confidence and low self-esteem.

- There might be additional difficulties with speech, motor skills, directional and spatial awareness and numeracy and also there could be visual anomalies (see the problems with visual discrimination etc. mentioned as factors in earlier years).

An example of how to use the above indicators in later identification
Lenny is 8 years 6 months old and has been assessed by an independent educational psychologist who measured his IQ as 'high average'. His Key Stage 1 SATs results were 2s and 3s except for writing and spelling which were 1. The following indicators can be noted:

- performance in literacy skills is at a lower level than could be expected from performance in other curriculum areas   :   yes and shows that he has good long-term global information for facts

---

- performance is often inconsistent varying from day to day : yes, he gets very tired

- performance is varied dependent upon the child's mood : doesn't appear so

- oral language is often at a higher level than written language : definitely

- reading is slow and lacking in fluency : is underachieving here and when he tries decoding this breaks fluency but he uses contextual clueing

- there are problems with phonic decoding and synthesis when reading : inefficient decoding skills (poor rhyming skills)

- there are problems with remembering core keywords both in reading and spelling : is acquiring a small sight word store for both reading and spelling

- memory problems show themselves both with factual retention and more global recall : poor short-term auditory memory but efficient long-term recall, has a better visual-verbal memory

- spelling is bizarre : some words

- words attempted for spelling contain incorrect letters and letter combinations for particular sounds : has started to use simple sounds for spelling but has problems with sequencing and directional confusion

- spelling is inconsistent with previously learnt words spelt both correctly and incorrectly in one piece of writing : yes

- there are problems with pronouncing : when younger
  multi-syllabic words

- emotional/behavioural behaviours : is poor at concentration
  become evident because of lack of   and settling down to work
  self-confidence and low self-esteem

- there might be additional difficulties : no speech problems but
  with speech, motor skills, directional   handwriting is very weak
  and spatial awareness and numeracy   and there is much
  and also there could be visual   evidence of visual
  anomalies   directional confusion

Because Lenny coped with reading at Key Stage 1 his problems didn't become evident until later. His progress will be carefully monitored and particular attention will be given to building up his better sight memory store for reading and spelling and helping him to become more fluent by using his contextual ability with first letter(s) clues. Direct teaching will be given to 'rationalise' his phonic decoding and encoding skills going back to short vowels with onset and rime activities and building up from that. His parents will be encouraged to play rhyming games and share read.

Identification in the secondary sector
Chapter 6 in the Code is entitled Identification, Assessment and Provision in the Secondary Sector and is very similar to the chapter on the primary pupil. Again it emphasises early identification and assessment, ongoing teacher observation and assessment, pupil performance as measured against the National Curriculum and the National Literacy and Numeracy objectives and the use of standardised screening and assessment tools.

As teacher awareness and knowledge of specific learning difficulties grows there should be fewer pupils entering secondary schools who have not been identified and helped during their primary school years. However, it should be recognised that the educational demands are different and more demanding, especially where examination courses are concerned, than those experienced in primary education. Thus some students who coped satisfactorily during these earlier school years might find their specific learning difficulties causing them particular problems in the secondary sector.

There are certain characteristics which can be given to secondary teachers in order to alert them to any possible specific learning problem. These are:

- problems with note taking either orally or from blackboards/OHPs;

- production of work takes a long time;

- problems with essay writing because of organisational difficulties (loses the thread of thought with points written in random order, difficulties in deciding what is relevant and what is irrelevant, cannot carry out a discussion or argument on paper);

- problems with written work for although it may show satisfactory content the spelling is particularly weak, the handwriting is poor, the work is presented untidily, words are simple and there is little or no sign of proof-reading;

- discrepancies shown between course and examination work;

- discrepancies shown between oral work and written work;

- apparent problems with memory and personal organisational skills (especially time allocation);

- problems with recall of words (especially technical ones or those connected with the particular course);

- problems with reading (in particular with coping with large amounts) and reading avoidance;

- problems in producing work at the expected level although apparently able and/or talented in certain areas.

It is not expected that all the above would be seen but subject teachers should be alert to any presenting problems.

An example of how to use the above indicators in secondary identification
Ben is 11 years 4 months old and although he had some minor literacy problems in the primary sector he entered his secondary school with adequate reading and writing skills. However, in the first few weeks his subject area teachers were concerned about his ability to access the curriculum.

* problems with note taking either : found this particularly
  orally or from blackboards/OHPs   difficult

* production of work takes a long time : very little work produced

* problems with essay writing because : yes
  of organisational difficulties

* problems with written work : spelling weak but
  readable but layout is
  untidy

* discrepancies shown between : not as yet seen
  course and examination work

* discrepancies shown between : he rarely answers orally
  oral work and written work

* apparent problems with memory : great problems here
  and personal organisational skills

* problems with recall of words : no real problems here

* problems with reading and reading : no problems here
  avoidance

* problems in producing work at the : homework never
  expected level although apparently   completed, avoidance
  able and/or talented in certain areas   techniques seen

When the co-ordinator of special needs observed Ben closely she found that his whole problems stemmed from an extremely weak auditory memory and weak listening skills which made it very difficult for him to listen to information, hold it, process it and recall it. His subject area teachers were asked to:

- give him instructions in small steps so that he completes one part of a task at a time;

- provide written or pictorial *aides-memoires* for reference;

- get him to repeat the activity to help hold and process the information;

- check his homework diary (he has to write the information correctly, understand what he has to do, complete the task satisfactorily, bring back the work to school, give it in).

Other 'criteria'

Definitions and identification of specific learning difficulties can also relate to the following terms: 'exclusion criteria', 'positive signs criteria' and 'discrepancy criteria'. These terms are often used to either confirm or reject identification of specific learning difficulties in the educational domain. Therefore, it is necessary to describe these but care and consideration has to be used when taking them into account because of all the problems that can arise.

Exclusion criteria

There is the possibility that learning difficulties occur because of other factors. These other areas which need checking are the medical areas of vision, hearing, speech, language, motor development and general health. Behavioural problems should also be noted. It should be stated that there are those educationists who feel that a child should not be labelled as having a specific learning difficulty if there have been problems such as:

- sensory impairment – vision/hearing problems (early or continuing);

- motor problems;

- language problems (low receptive language skills – understanding);

23

- physical problems such as difficulties with fine motor skills;

- health problems especially if these result in much absence;

- pre-school and continuing behavioural problems;

- frequent changes of school, inappropriate teaching, lack of early schooling;

- emotional problems (poor self-image/lack of motivation);

- environmental circumstances (problems at home/parental pressure);

- English as a second language.

The above list forms the exclusionary criteria which states that other causes of the learning difficulty should be excluded before the specificity of the problem can be determined.

However, it should be said that it is not really helpful to discuss this debate in any detail because if children have a learning problem one needs to help them overcome it. It can be pointed out that if the literacy (and/or any other learning) difficulty rapidly improves when any of the above problems are resolved and a structured programme of work is given then the original learning problem was possibly not long-term and, therefore, had its root in the 'other' problem. Here the threshold approach should be helpful (see Classroom Strategies) in order to see whether help and support need to be given just for a short period of time or whether it is really long-term and intractable and, therefore, by definition 'specific'. This approach should also help schools determine the level of support that should be given.

Discrepancy criteria

The Code of Practice (1994) seemed to imply that there have to be extreme discrepancies between how the pupil performs on 'appropriately administered standardised tests of cognitive ability or oral comprehension' and how the pupil performs on 'appropriately administered standardised reading, spelling or mathematics tests'. It can be a problematic road to follow if one tries to compare attainment with likely capabilities. It is sensible to treat and interpret all scores with care but to use diagnostic tools in depth. The Code of Practice (2001), although stating that 'academic attainment is not in itself sufficient for LEAs to conclude that a statutory assessment is or is not necessary', continues in para. 7:40 to infer that 'attainment is the essential starting point when considering the evidence'. This section is more general than the previous Code as it covers all areas of need.

Therefore, where statutory assessments requests are concerned it would appear that LEAs will ask for the discrepancy model to be carried out and the results used, alongside other areas, which will be discussed later in this book and particularly in IEPs and Specific Learning Difficulties.

Core subjects of the National Curriculum

When schools have to provide evidence for the LEA when statutory assessment is requested they have to provide information about the child's attainment in the core subjects of the National Curriculum measured against each other to see if there are extreme discrepancies. In practice this generally means that the overall level for English is low while that for mathematics and/or science would be average or higher than average. However, one should be aware that some pupils may gain a below average level in mathematics because of dyscalculia or if SATs levels are used there may have been problems with the reading side to the questions. (When SATs take place readers are permitted for mathematics and science and teachers should do their best not to penalise pupils with specific learning difficulties by insisting that they complete these papers unaided.)

The core language subject (English/Welsh)

Also connected with the National Curriculum the child's attainments within one core subject (in particular English/Welsh) have to be seen to be discrepant. In practice this would mean that a child's level in Attainment Target 1 (speaking and listening, oral in Welsh) would be at an average or above average level whereas Attainment Targets 2 and 3 (reading and writing) would be below average. Because specific learning difficulties do not fit into convenient patterns there may be some pupils who would have problems with expressive language as has been mentioned previously.

Intelligence

Another area dealing with the discrepancy model concerns the pupil's intelligence or cognitive ability. A consensus among those who have taught and observed the pupil should alert teachers and the LEA that the pupil's expected actual performance in National Curriculum assessments and tests is discrepant. This should be supported by standardised assessments 'as can reliably be administered'. Although cognitive assessments are not mentioned within para. 7:40 the terms 'psychometric tests' and 'cognitive development including reasoning, organisational and problem-solving skills' are referred to in *SEN Toolkit*, Section 8: Guidelines for Writing Advice. There is the danger of subjective assessments being made in this area of intelligence with teachers and/or parents/carers believing that the pupil is more intelligent than academic or literacy tests imply. This can favour the articulate pupil with specific learning difficulties who is well able to express him or herself. Often it is not until an educational psychologist administers either the WISC (Wechsler Intelligence Scale) or BAS (British Abilities Scale) intelligence tests that a truer indication of the child's cognitive ability becomes apparent. However, different tests bring different results and reading tests assess different areas of literacy. This is discussed in the chapter on Assessment.

But there are limitations to intelligence tests and the scores need not be fixed throughout the child's life although in practice they tend to show similar results if reteested over a period of time. If one considers an IQ score of 100 and a 10-year-old pupil, one could expect a reading and a spelling age of 10 years. If this IQ score was 120 then on this basis one could expect a reading and a spelling age of 12 years. If the discrepancy criteria is brought into play a 10-year-old with an IQ of 120 and reading and spelling ages of 8 years could be said to have disparities between the two scores which to some people would be very worrying. If this child had reading and spelling ages of 10 years, at age-appropriate level, would similar concerns exist? There is still a discrepancy. The word 'significant' can cause problems as its meaning cannot be readily understood or determined. Psychologists have 'significant criteria' built into their tests so that they are able to work out how scores match each other. For the non-psychologist using other methods of assessment, it is more difficult to determine what can be deemed as significant or what can be said is severe or what could be said would be within the normal expected range. Teachers may have to use their subjective judgements or wait for psychological help.

Positive signs criteria

This method of identification assumes that there is measurable or discernible evidence which determines the presence of specific learning difficulties. Checklists have been devised which give such indicators as have already been mentioned. Often these form a list asking, for example, for signs of directional confusion, inability to sequence and recite the days of the week or months of the year, showing signs of cross-laterality, difficulties with tying shoelaces or standing on one leg, problems with learning tables and producing spelling which is bizarre. However, it is not helpful to use tick lists for identification purposes as many children who can access the curriculum areas well and who can read and spell adequately also could show themselves to be positively 'dyslexic' in some respect. Also there are often no accepted number of positive indications built into these checklists which would confer what would deem one person to have specific learning difficulties and another to be within the accepted learning range.

The Code of Practice (2001) also uses the term 'identifiable factors that could impact on learning outcomes' within its general section on application for statutory assessment as did the previous Code. These include:

'Clear, recorded evidence of clumsiness, significant difficulties of sequencing or visual perception; deficiencies in working memory; or significant delays in language functioning.'

(para. 7:43)

It is interesting to note that although these are general they fit well within the specific learning difficulties category but could also indicate that these are problem areas found within other categories of learning need.

Learning difference

Identification can present many problems to both parents/carers and teachers. The consultation document, *SEN Thresholds*, attached to the draft Code (2000) provided a set of criteria which was based on more than just the discrepancy model. Positive signs (identifiable factors in childrens' learning) were also discussed. It is important to gather as much evidence as possible to indicate levels of difficulty and areas of strength. Often teachers are able to look back into the child's educational history for information and then feel they have found reasons for the learning problem. In this way they use the exclusionary criteria. When a child begins to fail to learn and one wants to know the reason for this it can also appear to be helpful to look to the so-called 'positive' signs and from these attach the label of 'specific learning difficulties'.

However, individuals have different styles of learning. They have their own strengths and weaknesses. These strengths and weaknesses may show up in global areas of learning or in very particular processes. Also individuals face up to their own problems in very different ways. Some have positive self-esteem and are confident in their own learning while others feel

27

themselves to be failures and their self-esteems are very low. Often their self-image matches how their parents/carers feel about the learning problem and, thus, it is important for parents/carers to be helped to come to terms with their child's specific learning difficulties (see the section titled Working with parents/carers).

To identify and then assess pupils correctly in order to help them overcome their problems teachers need to know how these children are 'learning different' and then to use the positive sides to advantage when setting up learning programmes. Identification may arise from any source but then the more detailed assessments have to be made in order to maximise efficient teaching and learning for individuals.

Assessment

It is important to be able to back up what one feels one has identified with some type of assessment technique which can be carried out within the school or with the help of external specialists.

Teacher assessment

Class teachers can start by using the child performance indicators that were mentioned in Identification. However, there are also criteria-referenced and standardised tests which can be used by the class teacher, the special educational needs co-ordinator (SENCo) and by advisory and learning support teachers. By using these means of assessment, more detailed records can be written about the pupil's strengths and weaknesses. A profile should be built up using these performance indicators, criteria-referenced assessments and/or standardised tests.

Criteria-referenced assessments

These assessments look at how the pupils perform at whatever they are asked to work on. They can be swift to use and most can be administered in the classroom rather than making an issue of extracting the child into a separate room. The teacher can diagnose where there are strengths and weaknesses within an area of skills and, therefore, will gain more insightful information in order to build up the pupil's profile. Check sheets can be used for recording such information.

In order to learn how to read and spell effectively the young child should be competent in particular areas. These are readily identifiable and there are criteria checks which can be easily made within the classroom situation:

- For the visual areas (visual perception, discrimination, sequencing, categorisation and memory):
  check with matching, 'odd one out', pictures, story sequencing, putting objects into categories and Kim's Game.

- For the auditory areas (auditory perception, discrimination, sequencing, categorisation and memory):
  check with phonological awareness activities such as rhyming activities, segmentation of words, beating the syllables in multi-syllabic words, giving similarities and differences in words, understanding of whispered blending, alliteration, onset and rime activities, the understanding of analogies (how one word can be changed to another by altering one or more letters).

- For fine motor control competencies (visual motor processing and handwriting):
  check with threading beads, colouring, drawing shapes, drawing a line between two lines, copying a few letters of the alphabet, hand control and pencil grip.

- For specialised word knowledge (positional words e.g. left/right/up/down, book words):
  check orally.

- For early number concepts:
  check with saying numbers 1–5, 6–10, 0 (when presented randomly) and writing these when asked, one-to-one correspondence.

- For adequate expressive and receptive language knowledge and usage:
  check with oral work in class.

- For the ability to understand, process and carry out spoken instructions:
  check with following simple instructions.

When looking at a child's performance in the literacy areas, depending on the age and attainment of the particular individual, the following skills and sub-skills can be checked:

- Reading:
  check through miscue analysis (plus the sub-skills of phonics, key words, phonological awareness, auditory and visual discrimination and sequencing).

29

- Spelling:
  check through miscue analysis (plus high frequency word knowledge, auditory and visual discrimination and sequencing).

- Writing:
  check from examples of independent writing (plus handwriting).

Reading

Miscue analysis forms the basis of reading assessment. Teachers have to determine how the pupil tackles unknown words and from this will be able to ascertain if he or she is a visual or phonic reader, if he or she tries unknown words or just waits to be told and whether contextual cueing is evident. When the child reads a passage that is slightly too difficult the substitutions for unknown words can be analysed as:

	Graphically correct	**Graphically incorrect**
Contextually correct	write the response under this column if the first letter(s) is the same as the original plus if the response fits the context of the sentence	write the response under this column if the first letter(s) is *not* the same as the original plus if the response fits the context of the sentence
Contextually incorrect	write the response under this column if the first letter(s) is the same as the original plus if the response does *not* fit the context of the sentence	write the response under this column if the first letter(s) is *not* the same as the original plus if the response does *not* fit the context of the sentence

An example of a miscue analysis
  Billy is 8 years 9 months old and the miscue analysis is taken from one of his chosen reading books which was above his readability level.

	Graphically correct	**Graphically incorrect**
Contextually correct	over/on spacesuit/spacecraft milk/milky Venice/Venus metal/meteor branch/balance use/using first/fastest spent/speed object/oxygen	
Contextually incorrect	break/bacon helent/helmet distance/direct stared/stray	injured/linger

  Apart from one non-word Billy's substitutions are real words and all but one starts with the correct letter. The majority of his substitutions are contextually correct. He seems to have a tendency to rush into words without checking so this can be worked on. He doesn't seem to be totally sure about using the correct first two letters so all the consonant blends and digraphs should be checked and some work given on these. He then should be helped to cope with two-syllable words.

Other criteria assessments for reading
  Diagnostic assessment can be obtained from:

- knowledge of the sets of basic core keywords (National Literacy Strategy) as sight words;

- knowledge of which individual letter sounds are known (consonants and short vowels);

- knowledge of other letter sound combinations (such as consonant clusters);

- blending ability (can the child blend from whispered heard sounds, can the child blend and synthesise three-letter regular words, cvc/consonant-vowel-consonant, and four/five-letter regular words);

- phonological awareness (such as giving rhyming words to a stimulus word, beating out syllables in words, understanding alliteration, word-sound association or analogies, giving particular sounds from beginnings, middles and ends of words);

- being able to hold sounds in the working memory and to repeat and/or blend them;

- being able to see differences and similarities between patterns and/or words, to find smaller words in longer ones.

An example of a pupil who has phonological problems in reading and is totally a visual reader

Kylie is 7 years 8 months old and is felt to be of generally average ability. She manages to remember the words from the reading scheme books but faced with unknown words she has no strategies for reading them. It was found that she had problems with:

- understanding the concept of rhyme;

- providing rhyming words to given stimulus words;

- beating the correct number of syllables in words;

- blending two letters as she wanted to add an 'er' to the end letter (e.g. 'aper' for 'ap');

- knowing all the initial consonant blends and short vowels;

- c-v-c (consonant-vowel-consonant) blending from whispered sounds (only slightly better with onset and rime);

- when given lists of similar-sounding words tended to perseverate by becoming muddled and jumping back to a previous list.

A very structured phonic programme was worked out for Kylie starting with oral work on sounds (games for the home etc.) and then three-letter word reading in two chunks (onset and rime). All work would be multi-sensory involving the use of plastic letters with much reinforcement. Reading through visual memory strategies would be continued.

An example of a pupil who has a very limited visual memory for core and high interest words but who can cope with the phonic side to reading
Dean is an 8-year-old highly verbal non-reader whose excellent vocabulary gets in the way of any effective reading as he wants to make core keywords more interesting (e.g. 'weird' for 'with'). He has many visual directional problems and knows that he has seen words before but he cannot recall the label. He knows very few of the first 100 keywords and finds reading scheme books very difficult. Because he is strong phonically he wants to sound out and blend every unknown word (sometimes this doesn't work as in 's-h-o-u-t-e-d' and sometimes he does so in a somewhat idiosyncratic way as in 'ch-h-ill/chill' and 'bl-l-ack/black').

To help Dean's self-esteem the phonic programme is to be emphasised so that he learns the consonant digraphs and blends and the more usual vowel digraphs. The Fuzzbuzz series of books will be given because of their phonic emphasis. However, in order to build up his core words he will be given these with pictograms so that there will be an added marker to help him.

Spelling
As with reading, a miscue analysis of written work can give far more information than just looking at words learnt for a spelling test. The tester is able to determine at which stage of spelling acquisition is the speller and whether the attempts show knowledge of serial probability (the letters that can be written together) in the English spelling system. One can also check for:

33

- knowledge of core sight words;

- the ability to produce letters for sounds (initial consonants and short vowels, then other regular sounds such as consonant clusters);

- the ability to spell regular phonemic words;

- being able to discriminate between similar sounds and being able to word-sound associate;

- the ability to see that words are similar or dissimilar and to be able to find small words in longer ones.

An example of an analysis of a pupil's independent written work in order to work out an appropriate spelling programme
Simone is 10 years 2 months old, reads well and copes with subject areas.

Reasonable		Unreasonable		Bizarre attempts		Auditory confusion Directional confusion	
poket	pocket	sidd	side	sed	scared	jrops	drops
gos	goes	kip	keep	pus ten	person	ofer	over
sum	some	don	down	masha	match	nufer	another
cud	could	lan	land	tus	touch	hafing	having
gardun	garden	wet }	went	wassed	washed		
mor	more	wen }		madr	?	bont	don't
rokit	rocket	mus	much	sau	?		
pepall	people	goin	going	wast	?		
buy	bye	frst	first	sotid	?		
wen	when	calld	called	fiming	?		
flor	floor	hoosing	housing				
cums	comes	flas	flash				
		riat	right				
		nir	near				
		sedi	said				
28%		*36%*		*24%*		*12%*	

(reasonable = letter patterns found in the English spelling system
unreasonable = some visual or phonemic attempts seen
bizarre = cannot be read by the reader)

Simone has many problems in the acquisition of spelling and her written work doesn't always communicate because she has many problems with the sound-symbol system. Because of her difficulties with medial consonants, word endings and auditory confusion she should be checked for any present or past hearing and speech problems. There are keywords incorrectly spelt so it is probably best to build up her common word knowledge by visual means before starting to build on her basic phonemic knowledge.

Apart from using pieces of independent written work for analysis there are passages for dictation that can be given. One set written for different levels or chronological age levels has been compiled by Margaret Peters.

An example of an analysis of a pupil's spelling using Peters' Diagnostic Spelling Assessment at the 9/10 years level
Michael is 13 years old with a spelling age of around 9 years but who can read well and cope with all the curriculum areas. After analysing his attempts (plus looking through his school books) the following conclusions were made:

- He writes very quickly but can read his own writing.

- He can generalise visually in order to cope with unknown words (e.g. his spelling of the words 'hele(copter)' and 'sight' from knowing 'television' and 'height').

- He has acquired a wide sight vocabulary of known words.

- He can 'hear' letters that he misses out of words when he goes over his errors.

35

- He has problems with syllabication and has his own ideas of seeing ways of splitting up words for learning purposes.

- He can use his intelligence for attempting some words.

- There are some problems with letter order and sequencing.

- Because of probable gaps in his phonic/phonemic learning he has missed out 'sound' letter patterns.

It was decided that he could cope with learning about the structure of words, such as prefixes, suffixes and word derivations so such a programme was set up.

Late one night my firend woke me saing would you enjoy a trail run in my new helecopter. I had scaresle scurmbled into my tracsuite before we were away. The ligths of the sitty gloed benith the stars above. I was beging to wonder about are distinasion when I cought sight of the sping nife edght and the surface of what must of been a tipe of flying surcer wisling round us. We doghed skillfully to advoud an acided. To are relif the space cared regained hight and we sanked down to earth and the curable bed I had neaver actaly lefted.

Writing (including handwriting)
If the pupil is able to write a sustained piece of work it can be useful for a 5–20 minute story or equivalent piece of writing to be analysed. Many skills can be observed such as:

- spellings;

- word usage;

- sentence construction;

- punctuation;

- amount of words attempted;

- presentation (including organisational skills).

36

An example of a child with spelling and handwriting problems
Steven is 10 years old with a history of spelling and fine motor control difficulties. He is left-handed and also has problems with spatial awareness. He works with an occupational therapist in order to help his hand control. He can learn words visually and he understands serial probability but he scans right to left and cannot pick out similar letter patterns in lists of words.

Example 1 at CA (Chronological Age) 7 years 3 months

... I ktepp and swimin and sem of the work and he pouy tim and goin on the Bkgeey and the ajietige ey

Example 2 at CA 8 years 4 months

I like siwing because if you ate hot it cools you down aia we do nice things in siwming. I can siwn 100 meatels and I can do all the stroke the only one - I can not do is buffely

Example 3 at CA 9 years 10 months

I like siwning because if you ate hot. it cools you down and we do nice things in siwning. I can siwn a 100 medlets and I can do all the stokes. The only onel can not do is Buffly

Example 4 at CA 11 years 1 month

I like Siwning Because if you ate hot it cools you down and we do nice thing in Siwnning. I can siw a 100 metbers and I can do all the the strokes. The only one I can not do is Butterfly.

It was originally felt that he may need to learn keyboard skills for word processing if his handwriting remained such a problem. However, after the final check it was felt that the handwriting programme was being successful and that he would be able to cope with the written work that was demanded in school. Where spelling is concerned he should work on visual patterning within words.

However, in order to analyse handwriting correctly the teacher has to observe the pupil actually writing because it is important to check the following:

- handedness;

- pencil hold;

- position when writing;

- position of the book or piece of paper;

- letter formation.

The above criteria-reference assessments can evolve over time. What is needed is that where a particular problem is found the teacher should try to see where this problem starts so that a programme is built from the earliest stage of difficulty. All information should be carefully recorded.

Standardised assessments

Assessments under this heading are those that have been given to a large number of the school population of varying ages in order to gain measured norms, standardised scores, percentiles or ages. Children's performances at tasks, such as reading and spelling, can be compared against those of their peers. General cognitive ability can also be measured. It has to be accepted that some standardised assessments are old and, therefore, norms might have changed over time. Scores from tests such as these should be sensitively taken into consideration.

Early years identification

Early identification using standardised assessment where specific learning difficulties are concerned is in its infancy but research is being undertaken by educationists. One such example is Dr Chris Singleton at Hull University.

Singleton's *Cognitive Profiling System* (*CoPS 1*) has been set up in order to tackle the problem of identification early in the child's life rather than waiting for the child to fail which might come much later in his or her educational career.

CoPS 1 is a computer programme of various sub-tests for use with children aged between four years and eight years which are administered on an individual basis in order to attempt to ascertain which children may experience problems with reading later on in their school life. From the profile printout teachers can see which of these pupils may have an associated specific or dyslexic problem as there are two sets of results, one visual and one auditory. His programme is not intended for labelling young children as 'dyslexic'. Rather the results will give a graphic profile of the child's cognitive strengths and weaknesses so that individual learning programmes can be devised and administered. Also it is intended that help can be given to eliminate the difficulty at an early stage, in fact before problems in the actual reading progress are experienced. So far encouraging results are being shown. (This research work has been extended to programmes for older pupils as well.)

Another such screening test which resulted from research is the *Dyslexia Early Screening Test (DEST)*, by Fawcett and Nicholson. This is a battery of ten sub-tests, suitable for children aged 4 and a half to 6 and a half years. Therefore, it overlaps with the early primary years. The items assess competence in phonological awareness, memory retrieval, fine motor skills, visual motor skills, postural stability and some knowledge of number and letter names. The results provide an 'at risk' quotient which can alert educators to those children who may have specific learning difficulties as they grow older.

Standardised assessment in the primary and secondary sectors

Linked with the last-mentioned screening test is the *Dyslexia Screening Test (DST)*. There are 11 sub-tests which have been developed for children aged six and a half to 16 and a half years. Some of the items are similar to those for the younger children, assessing competence in memory retrieval, fine motor skills and postural stability. Others assess areas within reading, spelling and verbal fluency. Again the results provide an 'at risk' quotient which can make the educators aware of those children who may have specific learning difficulties.

Non-verbal performance testing

Group tests have been devised to look at this area of children's performance, many of which are published by NFER.

There are fewer opportunities for individual assessment in this area. One of these is Raven's Progressive Matrices which is said to be a test of observation and clear thinking with two separate tests of matching patterns (Raven's Coloured Progressive Matrices for children up to 11 years and Raven's Standard Progressive Matrices for six years up to adults). It is an untimed test so this is an advantage for children who need time to think things out. It does not give an IQ score although it provides information on a pupil's ability to think clearly and logically.

Verbal performance testing

Also within the batteries of group tests are verbal assessments. Again information can be gained from NFER, and again there are fewer that assess on an individual basis.

As part of the Raven's Matrices there are also vocabulary scales (Crichton and Mill Hill Vocabulary Scales) which provide information on the pupil's ability to give word definitions. They are essentially oral assessments and, therefore, they complement the matrices tests. There can be interesting differences between the scores on the two sets of tests.

Another individual assessment of language is the British Picture Vocabulary Scales which is an assessment of the individual's received language or understanding of given words. The pupil is presented with many pages containing four pictures on each and the tester gives one word (either a label or concept) and the pupil has to point to what is known to be or thought to be the correct picture. Scores are given as standardised and percentile scores and age equivalents can be given. It is said that scores on this test often correlate well with the Verbal IQ score on the WISC tests.

Reading tests

Standardised tests of reading are very varied. They can be group or individual assessments and can range from single word tests through to sentence and passage reading assessments. Some are now quite old and because reading tests are used in different ways it is most important to read the manuals before use. Reading tests can give information on reading ages, standardised scores or percentile ranks. Sometimes it may be felt to be necessary to show the discrepancy between actual age and reading age. This is particularly so if one wishes to match the readability and interest levels of reading books with the reader. However, it is more important to analyse how a reader accesses the text (see below for an explanation of miscue analysis).

Passage reading

A miscue analysis of how a child reads can be accomplished through the passage reading tests such as the Revised Neale, the New Reading Analysis (readability 6.9 onwards) and the Individual Reading Analysis (for the early years reader). These tests are a range of graded passages which do not produce a reading age but a range of two scores between which the reader's competence at reading lies. The passages are not meant to be read without the tester noting how the pupil accesses the passages as a miscue exercise.

There are also comprehension questions which produce scores showing how the reader understands the texts. The Neale tests require these questions to be answered from memory which can either throw light on a pupil's memory capabilities or can give a false indication of the pupil's underlying ability if the pupil has a very poor retentive auditory memory but fundamentally excellent understanding. Testers should be aware of this when using this test on pupils with specific learning difficulties who have particular problems with their working memories. The other two assessments allow the pupils to refer back to the passages which give the tester indications of whether the pupil uses study skills of skimming, scanning, rereading or use of picture clues.

An example of a miscue analysis for the Individual Reading Analysis X (the first three passages)

Kenny is 8 years 2 months old and it is very difficult to help him acquire the skills for reading because he has very poor visual and auditory memories.

The house was dark.
The man went in.
    men
He   did   not come out.
His/he b/d-id/did

Pat   has   an old book.
Pet/Pat heard   boot/d-ook
She looks at it when   she is   sad.
           w-h-em   was

The ship   was in dock.
  sh-ip/ship   doot/dook/dop.
A girl   ran on to the   deck.
 g/girl r   in   a/the beek/beck/beach.
She hid in a big box
       book
and was still there when the ship left.
   sht   lit/la

Kenny has gaps with his keyword knowledge and he has some visual directional confusion. He has some knowledge of reading for meaning and some rudimentary knowledge of phonic decoding. Although these passages were too difficult he didn't give up. Because it seems that he could cope more easily with phonics a simple phonic programme is being set up.

An example of a miscue analysis for the New Reading Analysis (the third passage from A)
Jenny is 9 years old and reading has always been a problem for her.

It was late at night and Alex was on her way home. The roads were

silent and empty and all the houses were dark. It was then she heard a
str   emp
tremendous noise above her. Alex looked up into the night sky. She
tend   nose about
could   hardly believe her eyes. Some kind of huge aircraft was
couldn't hear bel   kid   hung   air
hovering above the town. It had flashing lights in many different colours.
hoving   about   flashed   much
What she saw next she would remember all her life.
                      wouldn't   left

Problems arise from four areas:

- sight memory for core words and other high interest words is still limited (she was more able to read keywords out of context);

- a visual reader who generalises from the shape of the word or part of the word;

- poor sight recall prevents efficient use of context;

- has some simple phonic decoding strategies (and is more confident decoding out of context).

It was decided that Jenny should read just at her independent reading level to give her fluency. Simple cloze procedure should be given to help her understand guesswork. Activities for core word retention such as 'find the word' will be supplied and the phonic programme will be continued and she will be encouraged to use this knowledge when she reads texts.

Miscue analysis

There are different approaches for teachers to take when undertaking a miscue analysis. For some it is helpful to note down in writing exactly what the child tries (as the above examples show) and then these can be analysed into the various strengths and weaknesses the child might have. From this information teaching programmes can be devised or altered. It can be advantageous if the passages are photocopied or marking sheets are used (as are supplied with these reading tests) for ease of recording. Also there are ways of using symbols that indicate how the reader attempted unknown words (such as 'sc' for 'self-correction' and circling any omitted word). Books listed in the References and Further Reading give examples of these.

Miscue analysis can only occur if the passages read are sufficiently demanding but not at frustration level where too many words are out of the child's knowledge. It can be more difficult to miscue when the child is reading his or her reading book where it would be hoped that this is at an appropriate level where only a few words are unknown. Some schools have banks of reading passages at varying readability levels which they will use half-termly with those pupils experiencing reading problems. In that way difficulties with texts are not associated with stories in books.

Single word reading

It is sometimes helpful to ascertain how a pupil copes with individual words. In order to be successful on such tests a pupil either has to know the words from sight or has to use phonic or generalisation skills in order to work out the unknown word. If pupils have problems with word-sound associations or with decoding and synthesising then individual word assessments like the NFER Graded Word Reading Assessment can be used to help with this information.

An example of how a pupil tackled single words on the NFER-Nelson Graded Word Reading Test
Word Card 1
Fay is 11 years 4 months old and there is some concern about her strategies for coping with unknown words. It is felt that her language knowledge is average.

The first ten words were correct.

barrow	bought	ridiculous	friction	critical
borrow	*brought*	*right/righteousness*		*ritral*

phantom	enraged	cubicle	relish	antiseptic
plantom	*enrage*	*cabile*	*relidge*	*antisipatic*

influenza	symmetrical	pedantic	vagrancy	client
infludent	*sImetri* (long 'i')	*ped*	*van*	*sil*

futile

futil (short 'u')

Fay is a visual reader who generalises from the shape of the word and who seems content to pronounce 'non-words'. There are some signs of former phonic decoding skills but she needs to learn how to break down multi-syllabic words and use competent strategies in synthesising them. It was felt that this could be organised through textual reading and from the errors that came from this.

Spelling tests
There are few recent spelling tests that give spelling ages and as with reading, although it is sometimes helpful to see the discrepancy between the pupil's actual age and spelling age, it is more helpful to use spelling assessments as diagnostic tools. Two examples of spelling tests that give spelling ages are Schonell Spelling Test and Young Parallel Spelling.

An example of a pupil's spelling when given the Schonell Spelling Test
Di is 11 years 1 month old and is being assessed at the beginning of her first term in the secondary school.

The first 30 words were spelt correctly.

sight	mouth	large	might	brought
site		*larged/large* (sc)	*mite*	*bought*

mistake	pair	while	skate	stayed
misstake/mistake (sc)	*paer/pear*	*wiyal/wieal*		

yolk	island	nerve	join	fare
yowck/yowk				*fair*

iron	health	direct	calm	headache
	heath	*b/diret/dierct*	*carm*	*headack*
		dieract		

Di seems to be using visual approaches where spelling is concerned. Although her spelling is fairly competent it was decided to put her into the school's spelling programme which would give her some awareness of phonemic letter strings.

Psychologist's assessment

Chartered educational psychologists either employed by the LEA or as private consultants usually administer the BAS (British Abilities Scale) or the WISC-R or WISC III (Wechsler Intelligence Scale for Children) battery of assessments in order to ascertain the child's cognitive ability.

The BAS is comprised of a number of sub-tests which assess various areas of cognitive performances. The WISC assessments are divided into two sections. One set of sub-tests makes up the Verbal IQ while the other set of sub-tests makes up the Performance IQ. The Full-scale IQ is based on scores from both sections.

Often children with specific learning difficulties have spiky profiles in that they score well on some sub-tests and poorly on others. Some psychologists and others concerned with dyslexia will look at the scores on four of the sub-tests: arithmetic, coding, information and digit span (which is termed the ACID profile) and if these are low in comparison with the other sub-test scores then it is felt that the child may be dyslexic. However, because children with specific learning difficulties differ in their intellectual profiles one should be wary of just using this information because the ACID profile is not always typical of a child with specific learning difficulties.

An example of a child's sub-test scores from the Wechsler Intelligence Scale for Children III Edition
Martin was 7 years 7 months old when this was given.

Verbal IQ 127 Centile 96		Performance IQ 97 Centile 42	
Information	12	Picture Completion	13
Similarities	18	Picture Arrangement	8
Arithmetic	9	Block Design	10
Vocabulary	18	Coding	8
Comprehension	15	Symbol Search	10

The conclusions were:

• above average for age for verbal ability;

• verbal reasoning, vocabulary and comprehension all excellent;

• significant discrepancy between verbal and performance scores which can lead to difficulties where self-organisation is concerned;

• dyslexic features present in terms of weak working memory and slow processing of symbolic information. Visual sequencing skills are also weak;

• specific learning difficulties are affecting acquisition of literacy skills.

Recommendations:

• extra support with self-organisation in class;

• acknowledgement of short-term memory difficulties and strategies given to help him process and carry out instructions;

• multi-sensory teaching to improve his reading and spelling attainments.

Educational psychologists are also able to use the assessment findings to predict the child's probable learning potential in reading and spelling and will work out how significant in statistical terms are the differences between measured cognitive ability and reading and spelling attainment scores. These measures can supply evidence when requests for statutory assessment using the criteria of the Code of Practice are sent in to LEAs.

SENCOs should be able to interpret and explain psychologists' reports to parents/carers especially when parents/carers feel that the numbers written down (IQ scores, potential scores, significance levels, spelling and reading ages) are more important than the diagnostic approach to assessment.

The Code of Practice and requests for statutory assessment

When a request is presented to the LEA from a school for consideration for statutory assessment the Code of Practice gives advice about the evidence to be provided (para. 7:13).

The first of these are the views of the parents/carers which have been recorded within school at the two stages, School Action and School Action Plus, plus copies of IEPs (individual education plans) at these stages. The pupil's views are also considered helpful if these are ascertainable. The school should also provide evidence of the pupil's rate of progress or lack of progress as measured over time. External evidence from other agencies should also be provided if these have been given.

However, there are no detailed guidelines for schools to consider when requesting a Statement for pupils with any particular learning need. However, there are generalised pointers which help to emphasise that pupils are unique and each one should be regarded separately. For example, within Chapter 7 of the Code of Practice (2001) the following paragraph entitled Cognition and Learning begins:

'Children who demonstrate features of moderate, severe or profound learning difficulties or specific learning difficulties, such as dyslexia or dyspraxia, require specific programmes to aid progress in cognition and learning.'

(para. 7:58)

This is, of course, very general as it covers all learning difficulties. However, the section continues by setting out the support requirements that pupils may require. The following appear to be those that would meet the needs of pupils with specific learning difficulties:

- Teaching arrangements should be flexible.

- Help should be given with memory difficulties.

- Help and support should be provided for the acquisition of literacy skills.

- Help is required with sequencing and organisational skills.

- Programmes need to be set up to aid improvement of fine and (gross) motor competencies.

(Adapted from para. 7:58)

The school would have to show that it had supported pupils who have been identified as having specific learning difficulties with the above particular problems. However, the Code points out that all pupils are unique and that their special educational needs might overlap the categories and unlike the previous Code it does not set out particular criteria for each special need. In fact in Chapter 7 the evidence requested about pupils' problems appears to be an amalgam of the previous Code's particular sets of criteria. Section 7 of the *SEN Toolkit* which is entitled Writing a Statement of Special Educational Needs is again a general document which gives advice about what evidence should be collected when a Statement is written.

However, because there are no direct details in the Code that discuss the particular needs of pupils with specific learning difficulties LEAs will probably work out their own set of criteria.

However, the Code of Practice (2001) has introduced School Action and School Action Plus to replace the three school stages in the five-staged assessment process in the previous Code. These stages will be discussed in the following chapter.

Classroom Strategies at School Action and School Action Plus

The Code of Practice (1994) suggested that schools followed a three-staged process for any child with a special educational need. Teachers working through these stages would use these to produce evidence of the problems and in-school ways of supporting and helping the pupil overcome them. The first involved the class/subject teacher and differentiated work. The second would bring in the support and advice of the SENCO and the setting up of IEPs while the third would invite others from outside the school to give extra advice. These other professionals could include educational psychologists, speech and language therapists, occupational therapists and advisory teachers.

The class teacher and differentiation

The previous Code established a Stage 1 which was involved with gathering basic information about the child's specific learning problem after either a parent/carer and/or teacher has expressed an initial concern. A first assessment of the problem would be made by the class teacher or tutor and '... *special help within the normal curriculum framework, exploring ways in which increased differentiation of classwork ...*' would be provided. The child's progress would be monitored and reviewed. Parents/carers would be kept informed at all stages and their advice and help asked for. The Code of Practice (2001) has dropped this stage. It is assumed that this has occurred because differentiation should be a focal point of all teachers' organisation. It is, however, necessary to mention the stage before the Code's School Action because there are pupils with specific learning difficulties who can be helped successfully by class/subject teachers' assessment and monitoring and differentiated procedures within teaching.

Class teachers in the primary school, especially in the early years, can use the lists already mentioned if they find that there is a pupil who seems unable to cope with the demands of the classroom.

Class teachers in the upper end of the primary school and secondary subject teachers will either have been given information about which pupils have specific learning difficulties before they teach the particular child or they will have queries about those pupils who appear to be finding the subject difficult. There are the factors to check from the lists previously given or this preliminary question can be posed in order to decide whether differentiated work is necessary:

- Are all the pupils acquiring the skills and knowledge that are intended from the particular lesson?

In order to answer that the teachers will have to check from:

- how the pupils answer orally;

- how the pupils react/function in whatever way they are requested;

- how the pupils appear to be listening;

- how the pupils produce written work;

- what is their general behaviour within the lesson.

This should give information that can be acted upon. Teachers could either immediately differentiate materials and/or change their own input to the lessons or the pupils' output. They could also share information with other members of staff to see if similar reactions occur in other lessons. Or they could contact the SENCO for extra support. This would start the School Action procedure which is when the pupil requires some type of intervention that is additional to or different from what is normally provided.

Differentiation can affect the way the teacher delivers the curriculum, the materials used, the organisational structure within the learning situation and the way the individual is able to access what is being taught and expected of him or her.

Young children can be grouped quite easily and those with problems in literacy skills can be given work adapted to their needs either with the class teacher or with a classroom non-teaching assistant.

Before the more formalised approach to teaching reading and spelling is undertaken work on early language skills should be given. These are detailed in books such as *Learning Difficulties in Reading and Writing – A Teacher's Manual* by Reason and Boot. Also ideas for activities and games can be found in the series of games and activity books for reading, spelling and language produced by NASEN among others. Much of the differentiated work in early years classes should be oral so that phonological awareness is built up and so that the pupils are able to cope with sequencing and discrimination skills in both the auditory and the visual modes.

Young children may need to make their own reading books or have these made for them. They will need to read and reread repetitive stories which they can memorise. Ideas for home-school liaison where reading is concerned can be found in many publications. Children may need someone to scribe their news and simple stories or to use sequencing techniques when words are written on sticky-backed cards.

As it will be noticed the suggested differentiated approach for children with suspected specific learning difficulties in the early years is no different from that for children with suspected general learning difficulties.

As children grow older and the work in the classroom becomes more demanding then differentiated work can be matched to individual needs. In brief children with recording problems may be allowed to use alternative methods such as producing diagrams and drawings or by one-word labelling. Tape recorders and/or word processing can be helpful. If reading is the concern then taped information might be provided or worksheets etc. might be rewritten to match the readability of the learner. Organisational and memory problems can be helped by *aides-memoires*, instructions given as written memos so the learner is not given an overload for retention purposes (short sentences used with repetition on behalf of both the teacher and the learner).

What has to be remembered is that children with specific learning difficulties, like any child with a special educational need, have the right to a broad, balanced curriculum and if they have problems in any particular area help must be given to alleviate these. It is implicit within all aspects of education that differentiation has to be used whenever a child has problems with curriculum access.

An example of a pupil who needs a differentiated approach and some in-class help with her literacy attainments

Sally at 8 years 10 months was noted to have some problems accessing parts of the curriculum because of parental concern about her reading and spelling attainments. It was noted that much absence had hindered her learning and she also changed schools in Key Stage 1. Glasses were recently prescribed. The class teacher checked Sally's reading on Salford B Sentence Reading Test and she scored a reading age of 7 years 10 months and her spelling scored at 7.1 years on Schonell Spelling Test. Sally's strengths were visual and although she knew her basic phonic skills she didn't use them in her reading.

In class she read daily to an ancillary who encouraged her to use phonic decoding and contextual strategies when she found she didn't sight recognise a word. Sally also worked in class with a small group of other pupils on a structured spelling programme.

At 9 years 10 months Sally was using all strategies within her reading which had increased to 9 years 2 months on Salford C and her spelling had improved to 7 years 10 months on Schonell. The programme was seen to have worked.

School Action and the involvement of the SENCO

School Action is mentioned in the sections concerning Early Years, the Primary Phase and the Secondary Sector in the Code of Practice (2001). Pupils are monitored, assessed and supported within class and if it is felt that the pupil continues to find accessing the curriculum difficult then there should be consideration of support at School Action. General triggers for this taken from the primary chapter which seem to pertain to specific learning difficulties are that the child:

- makes little or no progress when teaching approaches (methods, materials) are adapted and targeted specifically for the individual's identified problem areas;

- shows indications of problems in developing literacy skills which results in poor attainments within certain areas of the curriculum;

- shows indications of problems in developing mathematical skills which results in poor attainment;

- exhibits continual emotional and behaviour difficulties despite being supported through the behaviour management programmes usually used within the school;

- has some sensory or physical difficulties which are not helped by the provision of specialist support.

(Adapted from para. 5:44)

The Code uses the same triggers for the primary phase and the secondary sector (para. 6:51) which may not be particularly helpful where the education of older pupils is concerned. Again it is important for schools to look at the individual needs of pupils rather than to use a detailed set of triggers. The draft Code (July 2000) with its attached *SEN Thresholds* was far more detailed and suggested certain criteria for lower levels of difficulty for specific learning difficulties. These were:

- *performance in most areas of the curriculum within the range which most pupils are expected to achieve, but performance in one or two other areas which is markedly lower (e.g. towards the lower end of the expected range);*

52

- *attainment in some specific underlying skills (e.g. spelling, handwriting, number, manipulative skills) which enables the pupil to function across the curriculum as a whole but which is beginning to interfere with their ability to progress as effectively as might otherwise be the case;*

- *failure to overcome these difficulties or raise performance in weaker curriculum areas despite the sort of good teaching within a differentiated curriculum which is effective in securing the pupil's progress in other areas;*

- *avoidance of, or frustration with tasks that require weaker skills to be used, despite a willingness to tackle other tasks.*

(para. 4:5)

However, as already mentioned the Code of Practice (2001) omits these so that schools can determine individual needs and organise intervention programmes accordingly.

The SENCO is involved at this stage and here some of the assessment procedures mentioned previously can be used so that a more diagnostic profile of the child can be built up and a learning programme devised. This would be written onto an IEP which would then be carried out, reviewed and monitored (see IEPs and Specific Learning Difficulties).

School Action Plus and the involvement of the 'specialist'

School Action Plus is also mentioned in the sections concerning Early Years, the Primary Phase and the Secondary Sector in the Code of Practice (2001). Pupils continue to be monitored and supported within class but if it is felt that the pupil persists in finding accessing the curriculum and learning particular skills difficult then there should be consideration of support at School Action Plus. This involves the involvement of external specialists as these can act as consultants and be a source for in-service training. General triggers for this stage taken from the primary chapter which appear to relate to specific learning difficulties are that the child:

- has continued problems in certain areas over a period of time and shows little or no progress;

- continues to work at National Curriculum levels 'substantially' below that which is expected of his or her peers;

- has continued problems with the acquisition of literacy and mathematical skills;

- exhibits continued emotional or behavioural difficulties which interfere with his or her own learning and that of others, despite being allocated an individualised behavioural programme;

- has sensory or physical needs which require advice or support from a specialist service.

(Adapted from para. 5:56)

As with School Action the Code uses the same triggers for the primary phase and the secondary sector (para. 6:64) which again is not particularly helpful where the education of older pupils is concerned. The higher levels of difficulty for specific learning difficulties as stated within the *SEN Thresholds*, which again have been omitted from the finalised Code, were:

- *weaknesses in underlying skills which make it difficult for pupils to access and progress within large areas of the curriculum; for instance, literacy performance in the first or second centile as measured by standardised tests which makes it very difficult for pupils to access written materials or perform writing tasks in any area of the curriculum;*

- *inability to overcome these weaknesses to any significant degree despite carefully targeted interventions;*

- *inadequacy of alternative skills and approaches to ensure progress across the curriculum; for instance, use of oral or graphic recording and presenting information which is too slow and limiting to allow progress;*

- *evidence of frustation and damage to self-esteem caused by these difficulties, sometimes leading to disengagement from learning, non-attendance and/or behavioural difficulties.*

(para. 4:5)

The SENCO continues to be involved at this stage but here external 'specialists' such as educational psychologists and members of LEA advisory and support services become involved. These educationists may carry out observations and more detailed assessments in order to give additional ideas for a teaching and learning programme which would be written onto the IEP. Similar reviews and monitoring of this programme would take place.

An example of a pupil placed on Stage 3 with reference to possible request for statutory assessment (which would be School Action Plus)
After school monitoring and support Liam was moved to a Stage 3 at CA 9 years 3 months and both an advisory teacher and an LEA educational psychologist became involved with assessments and planning learning programmes. After the first review when Liam was 10 years 1 month it was felt that there was enough evidence to request statutory assessment.

- IQ was at the average level (WISC Full Score 96) with his non-verbal abilities slightly higher than his verbal abilities whereas his attainments in reading and spelling were particularly weak. As measured on Salford Sentence Reading Test C his reading age was 6.8 years (a probable over-estimate as he couldn't score on MIRA X). On Schonell Spelling Test his spelling age was 6.0 years;

- visual perception was very weak;

- visual and auditory memories were particularly limited;

- concentration span was limited and he could be both distracted and could cause distraction if confronted with work he couldn't cope with. He needed much individual help;

- the school had helped him access the curriculum by differentiating as much as possible;

- structured programmes of work as suggested by the LEA advisory staff were carried out within the school by his class teacher and learning support staff. This was learning keywords for reading and spelling, reading Trog books with 'easier' extra books written by the advisory teacher, doing oral work on sounds but not beginning more formal phonic work until some individual help could be provided;

- parental involvement and back-up of work at home is carried out.

Liam's case was discussed by the LEA panel and a statutory assessment was initiated.

In-class or out-of-class programmes at School Action and School Action Plus

It is expected that work programmes from the IEPs would be carried out in the normal classroom setting but there may be times when small group or individual teaching would be appropriate. This type of organisation would depend on the staffing of particular schools and whether there were extra support staff, either teachers or non-teaching support assistants, who could be allocated to undertake this work. Liaison with parents/carers is most important here.

Larger primary schools and secondary schools may find it easier to group-teach children with learning problems. If extra literacy support is to be given there is then always the dilemma of which subject areas could be 'missed'. Also from an organisational point of view it could seem expedient to teach pupils with specific literacy difficulties alongside those with problems of a more generalised nature. However, because of the former's particular needs and the latter's probable slower rate of learning from an educational point of view this is not the most advantageous way of working.

There are programmes published for group work which if used as stated could be beneficial for children with specific learning difficulties. Examples of these are *'Letterland'*, *'Alpha to Omega'*, *'Attack'* and *'Spelling Made Easy'* for spelling and *'Distar'* for reading. Reading schemes such as *'Wellington Square'* and *'Crown'* are frequently used but it should be remembered that these were not written for those with specific learning difficulties.

Multi-sensory teaching approaches

Individualised programmes that purport to be multi-sensory are various (and a brief explanation of a multi-sensory teaching approach can be found below), and which endeavour to find ways of tackling reading, spelling, handwriting and organisational problems. An often used programme is the one Kathleen Hickey devised. Many of these can begin in the primary sector and continue into the secondary sector because of their cumulative learning approach. It is important that for many pupils these programmes as well as being multi-sensory should be well-structured, sequential and containing a phonic component.

Because of children with specific learning difficulties having problems with auditory and visual sequencing, with synthesising of stored information and with working memory, it can be difficult to use solely a visual or an auditory method when teaching literacy skills. Even combining these may not succeed because the extra sensory systems of tactile-kinaesthetic (using touch and action) are required in order to produce the multi-sensory approach.

This approach co-ordinates the interaction of the senses of seeing, hearing, speaking and doing. It integrates the pupil's visual, auditory, oral and kinaesthetic capabilities. Programmes using these methods start at the base line of the child's knowledge which is why detailed assessment is necessary in order to determine what the child can or cannot do. The teaching programme then builds on this knowledge slowly and cumulatively. Each newly learnt process has to be thoroughly gone over until it becomes an automatic process. Once this occurs the next stage in the structured process can be taught.

As well as detailed assessment procedures being undertaken before the programme starts it is also important to record everything that is taught and learnt and periodically to revisit past processes to see that these have not been forgotten. It is essential not to rush any stage in the learning and, therefore, it is fundamental to let both the pupil and the parents/carers understand why such programmes are being used.

A basic example of learning through a multi-sensory approach: Acquisition of letter names and sounds

It can be seen that the processes overlap and are not intended to be carried out as separate functions.

1. The particular letter to be taught will be named and given its usual sound by the teacher. The child will listen using his or her aural processes.

2. By looking at the shape of the letter he or she will bring visual processes into play.

3. He or she will repeat the name and sound (thus again listening), so working in the oral mode.

4. A wooden or plastic letter shape can be felt using the tactile approach.

5. The pupil can write or make the letter shape employing the kinaesthetic mode (again saying the name and sound).

These five processes will help to fix the name and the sound and how to write the particular letter into the memory.

Words for reading and spelling can be dealt with similarly. The teacher will write and say the word which will be looked at and repeated. Plastic or wooden letters can be used to make the word with the cue and then without the cue. The whole word or even the separate letters can be spoken while this is happening. In the end the child writes the correct word on cue or reads it when it is presented.

If the identified problems are not as basic or entrenched as to need total multi-sensory approaches then modifications to the above can be made. As has been stated teaching should always try to match the child's strengths and weaknesses. Therefore, they will reinforce and consolidate what is known and thus become a positive reinforcement to the learning situation. They will augment what is not known in order to develop what could be the problem areas. In this way children with problems in the visual or auditory modes can be taught more easily through the preferred manner and can have the area where there is uncertainty and problems built up as a supplement.

The maxim to follow is to know the problem areas in as much detail as possible and to match the teaching and learning requirements to them.

Strands of action to meet special educational needs

A four-sectioned table is included in the *SEN Toolkit* Section 6: Strands of Action to Meet SEN (page 5), which is intended to help schools use different forms of action as intervention and support for pupils with special educational needs. It has been produced from research carried out on SEN thresholds undertaken in the University of Newcastle. The grid's sections are 'assessment and planning', 'grouping for teaching purposes', 'human resources' and 'curriculum and teaching methods'. It is pointed out that pupils may be working at different points on each strand at different times, within different contexts and during different lessons. The suggestions are general in nature as they cover the support required for all types of special educational need but they could become a useful resource for schools to determine the degree of severity which pupils might be encountering within their everyday lessons.

Assessment ranges from in-class appraisement, to the setting of IEPs, the involvement of external services to longer-term planning for the required provision. Grouping relates to pupils working within the ordinary classroom through to small group or individual support. Human resources extends from the pupil being taught by class/subject teachers, to the involvement of the SENCO, being given ad hoc and specialist advice and being supported or taught by someone with a specialism. Curriculum and teaching methods begin with differentiation and finish with specialised equipment. Nowhere in this section of the *SEN Toolkit* do its authors recommend whether a particular strand should meet a pupil's needs within School Action or School Action Plus or even for those pupils who have a Statement of Special Educational Need but its introductory page points out that the actions 'may be appropriate' for these. This page also points out that although most extra help will be given within classrooms any time spent outside these must be within the 'context of the inclusive curriculum'.

Literacy skills teaching

There is no particular order for teaching literacy skills with individuals or small groups if teachers are to devise the programme themselves. (Published programmes have their own particular sequences.) However, one could look at the following to determine where to begin such a programme:

Reading

- teaching of common core sight words (e.g. the NLS core words) (*These can be taught as flash cards, on probes, in sentences or found within other types of reading material*);

- the building up of sight vocabulary (high interest or subject-specific words) (*Structured reading schemes can be used, e.g. 'Wellington Square' or 'Crown', or particular words pertaining to a subject area can be taught as whole word entities*);

- the acquisition of reading techniques such as contextual cueing, reading on and returning, cloze procedure;

- teaching of letter sounds and phonic decoding (*working through the short vowels and consonant-vowel-consonant words, to consonant clusters, to regular endings such as 'ink/and/ent' etc., to words with the modifying 'e' ending, to common vowel clusters such as 'ar/or/er' and more irregular vowel clusters such as 'ow/ou/au' and harder units of sound such as 'ought/ight/ear/air'*);

- structured phonic-based reading schemes can be used (such as '*Fuzzbuzz*');

- multi-syllabic word attack skills
  (including syllabication and the understanding and synthesising of syllables and knowledge of prefixes and suffixes);

- higher reading skills
  (such as reading for meaning, reading between and beyond the lines, skimming, scanning, researching).

Spelling

- sight word spelling of common core words
  (using the visual approach advocated by Peters and Cripps in 'Catchwords', using the methods of Look, Remember, Cover, Write, Check plus Say in order to cover all the senses in a multi-sensory approach and/or Simultaneous Oral Spelling techniques, see Appendix 5);

- phonemic spelling strategies
  (using letters and letter combinations to attempt unknown words);

- understanding serial probability
  (which letters can be used together in the English spelling system and checking the phonemic attempts with visual memory for self-correction);

- proof-reading and dictionary skills
  (which could include the use of the specialised ACE Dictionary and Spellmasters and/or spellcheckers on word processors).

Handwriting

- correct letter formation
  (coupled with holding the writing instrument correctly and sitting in an appropriate position);

- cursive writing.

Written work

- generation of ideas and being able to use these to write a beginning, the body of the text and a conclusion
  (some tips for this can be found in 'Learning to Learn' published by NASEN);

- correct punctuation and grammatical accuracy.

If teachers are able to work out the individual programmes then they are not tied to anything published and can, therefore, meet the needs of the particular pupil.

The *SEN Code of Practice* (2001) and teaching requirements

The Code makes some statements relating to teaching but unlike the previous Code they are not as prescriptive and are, in fact, mostly general in order to cover all the range of special educational need. The Code, in sections 5 and 6, carries the same paragraph headed 'Nature of intervention' where one-to-one teaching is mentioned as are group or individual support, the provision of different learning materials and the possible provision of additional adult support time for 'devising the nature of the planned intervention and to monitoring its effectiveness'. Paragraph 7:58, as has already been mentioned, requires that 'flexible teaching arrangements' should have been in operation if a request for statutory assessment is made by a school for a particular pupil.

The Thresholds addition to the draft Code included a section, 4:7, headed 'Relating action to levels of special educational need' which states that pupils experiencing specific learning difficulties should be working within the ordinary classroom using those resources and strategies that are available. If pupils do not progress adequately then a review of these strategies should be made and there is reference to the statement on inclusion in the National Curriculum handbook. The previously mentioned table of strands of action is to be found here but in this case an extra section indicating the threshold has been added. The more detailed descriptors appertaining to specific learning difficulties and the case histories given have not been reproduced in the Code of Practice (2001) or within the *SEN Toolkit*.

Support in the secondary classroom

This support work can be carried out by teaching assistants, members of the special needs department, subject specialists who have been given special needs responsibility and members of staff who have time on their timetables. Unless this support is given specifically for a pupil with specific learning difficulties who has a Statement then help is often spread around all pupils who have learning difficulties. Subject teachers should be made aware that these two categories of pupils learn in different ways and at different rates and that grouping them together may not be the best type of organisation. The pupil with specific learning difficulties should be an integral member of the class but his or her particular problems should be known and noted.

Pupils with specific learning difficulties can be assisted in the following ways:

- Worksheets can be specially prepared to take account of particular problems.

- Specialised or technical vocabulary can be taught prior to the lesson (both reading and spelling).

- Help can be made available with the organisation of written work (e.g. mind-mapping, brainstorming, webbing).

- Preparation of written and/or tape-recorded notes can occur.

- The facility can be organised for the pupil to tape-record information.

- Assistance can be given in transcribing from the pupil's dictation and/or helping write up the tape-recorded information.

- The facility can be organised for the pupil to word process and be helped with this (tuition and support).

- Direct teaching, if appropriate, can help with understanding and learning particular skills and concepts for the subject.

An example of a secondary-aged pupil with a Statement of Special Educational Needs who is well able to give his own perceptions of his problems and his needs

Sam is 13 years 4 months old and at an Annual Review said that his problems were:

- that he had difficulties in all aspects of written work because of only being able to write extremely slowly (both in school and for homework). Copying from the board was particularly difficult as he was too slow to finish what he should do;

- that in spelling he made many mistakes when he was writing information etc. and was not able to concentrate on how to spell correctly;

62

- with self-organisation as his memory was weak (already he had lost two locker keys);

- in speed reading because although he can read quite competently he cannot skim and scan;

- with maths as although he felt he knew how to cope with certain aspects he was too slow and things took a while to sink into his brain;

- with concern about future examinations as he doesn't think he'll cope at GCSE level with all subjects. He feels that A-level work will be easier.

Sam's strategies so far include using a small tape recorder for both homework and classwork but this makes him appear different from his peers. He uses a small Spellmaster and has access to a personal computer at home although as yet his keyboarding skills are not particularly good. He gets a lot of parental support.

It was felt that Sam also needed a personal weekly timetable setting out books/equipment for his daily lessons. Staff needed to be aware of his slow processing and to make allowances for this. Wherever possible he would be given copies of notes rather than being expected to copy these himself and while others were employed with this he would be given extra time for completion of classwork. They would also check his homework diary to see that he had the correct information. He was allocated one lesson of support teaching where the emphasis would be on higher reading skills, study skills, hints on how to write essays and projects. There would be some reinforcement of spelling 'rules'. At home help would be given with keyboarding skills.

Special provision in examinations
Not all pupils with specific learning difficulties will need or even benefit from special provisions in public examinations. Nor is a Statement of Special Educational Need required before these are granted (at the time of updating this book). However, if it is felt that a pupil may not do him or herself justice in examinations then schools should look into putting special provisions into practice. Parents/carers should also be involved in any discussion about the need for special provisions.

Some pupils will cope during lessons but not during examinations. Problems in spelling, reading fast enough to extract relevant information and writing fast enough to produce enough work may present the pupil with extra stress. Just to know that extra time will be allocated may alleviate these feelings.

A recognised educational psychologist is required to write a report for pupils who are deemed to have specific learning difficulties within a period of 18 months prior to the examinations. There is usually a standard form which has to be filled in although examination boards can differ in their requirements so schools via the examination officer or special needs co-ordinator need to find out exactly what evidence is required to support any application for special provisions. Often what is needed is discrepancy between reading age and cognitive ability and reading and writing speeds. The assessment has to be carried out using standardised reading and spelling tests.

As well as extra time, up to 25% extra, some pupils with specific learning difficulties may be entitled to an amanuensis (a scribe or reader), tape-recording, working on a word processor and concessions for poor spelling. However, it has to be proved that the pupil's main mode of working is dictating or word processing if that is the provision requested.

The final certificate will be endorsed if the examination board has not been able to judge the spelling, punctuation and grammar of the individual which would occur if an amanuensis was used. It would have to be decided by both the pupil and parents/carers if this was a preferred option.

IEPs and Specific Learning Difficulties

Individual Education Plans continue to be requirements for School Action and School Action Plus and for the pupil who has a Statement of Special Educational Need. These are documents that outline the child's problems by stating long-term goals and short-term targets in order to help overcome these. They are working documents and should be used for planning, teaching and reviewing progress. When writing IEPs teachers have to state who will carry out the teaching programme and what materials and/or methods etc. will be used. A review date has to be stated and the parents/carers should know what the plans are. There should be a section for recording the outcome of progress made.

The Code gives some advice about IEPs and stresses that they should be 'crisply written and focus on three or four individual targets ... that match the child's needs' (para. 5:51). Teachers are reminded that because there is a differentiated curriculum plan in place then the targets should be 'additional to' and 'different from' what is written on this. It is also recognised that group education plans can be put into place.

Section 5: Managing Individual Education Plans in the *SEN Toolkit* is a useful document which provides useful advice about working with IEPs. This is far more detailed than the Code and it is practical in its approach. One message that is emphasised is that IEPs should be 'manageable' for those who use them as part of the intervention strategies set up to help pupils with special educational needs. The targets set should be 'achievable' so that the pupil's success can be discernible to all concerned.

When filling in IEPs teachers should answer these key questions:

- WHAT?   these are the particular targets that are stated for each pupil after assessment and consultation;

- HOW?   this would state the methods of teaching/supporting;

- WHICH?   this would state the materials to be employed;

- WHO?   the adult(s) involved (with parental liaison and back-up);

- WHEN?   the day(s) of the week and the particular times;

- WHERE?   the room (either in or out of the classroom);

- WHAT?   the success criteria (in order to evaluate if the programme has been successful);

- HOW?   the method of recording progress made.

A hidden question, but one that needs to be kept at the back of the mind, is WHY? Answering this gives the rationale behind the IEP for the particular individual.

Sometimes teachers want to put too many targets into a programme and then find that it is not manageable and nothing gets completed satisfactorily. When writing targets the teacher should consider the following suggestions:

- Do not state more than two targets in each skill area.

- Do not try to work on more than is achievable (others can be added when the first are successful).

- Use an active verb which is in the future tense.

- Write the targets in factual objective terms.

- Try to ensure that the targets can be achieved but make them challenging.

- Try to make sure that the outcomes can be measured.

- Relate outcomes to knowledge and skills.

- Relate outcomes to the assessment criteria.

An example of an Individual Education Plan for a child on Stage 3 (which has how become School Action Plus)

Stage 3: IEP   Date opened: September 14th 1995

Name: Danny W.
d.o.b.: 13th June 1986

Strengths: Verbally able, practical and artistic. Has a good grasp of general knowledge and has a lovely personality.

Concerns (attach previous IEPs and any other relevant information)
Reading is improving but there are gaps in his decoding skills. Great problems with spelling, seems unable to remember core words or to see similarities in words with same patterns.

Long-term aims: 1. To teach him the more common word
                        patterns which include vowel clusters so
                        that his reading reaches his age level.
                     2. To enable him to communicate with his
                        written work.

TARGETS	ACTION/PROGRAMME	SUCCESS CRITERIA
1. To teach him word endings such as 'ear/ain/out/own/ light' etc.	Worksheets and word lists	90% accuracy when working on the lists/ use in unseen reading
2. To spell correctly the three/four-letter words from the NLS lists	NLS lists with SOS and use of mnemonics	80% accuracy when reviewed
3. To use appropriate sound-symbol correspondence when writing own words	Check knowledge of basic sounds - work on three-letter words (then with four, consonant clusters) - use multi-sensory approaches	Unknown words in own writing showing signs of phonemic structure

Adults supporting the programme: School's support teacher working on 2/3 with back-up from special needs support assistant. Class teacher working on 1. Parents backing up 2 and working on sound games (also hearing reading).

Time and place: Two 15-minute individual sessions on Mon./Thurs. with the support teacher - three 15-minute back-up in class with the support assistant - daily reading to the class teacher - daily work at home.

LEA staff involved: LEA advisory teacher to review and advise.

Monitoring and review arrangements and date of next review: Advisory teacher to review in late Nov. School to monitor each month. Review with parents December 10th 1995.

The *SEN Toolkit* and the Code of Practice (2001) both use the same set of statements to state how progress can be measured. These can be summarised as progress that:

67

- helps to make less extensive any attainment gap between that of the pupil and his or her peers;

- helps to stop that gap growing wider;

- helps to increase the pupil's previous rate of progress;

- secures access to the curriculum;

- shows an improvement in the pupil's behaviours;

- enables the pupil to gain appropriate accreditation.

(para. 6:49)

For pupils with specific learning difficulties both parents/carers and pupils generally want to see an increase in literacy skills and attainment because these will enable better curriculum access. Those pupils with higher cognitive abilities also want to be able to cope with the examination system which will enable them to enter further or higher education.

The Statement

Some reference to what evidence the *SEN Code of Practice* (2001) expects schools to provide for the LEA if statutory assessment is requested has been given throughout the chapters of this book so far.

In the Code paragraphs 7:38 to 7:45 there is a section titled 'Evidence of attainment' which delineates the types of information the LEA would require. Although academic attainment is important it is pointed out that this attainment must be recognised within several contexts, peer attainment, rate of progress over time and expectations of performance, where this is thought to be relevant. Paragraph 7:40 requests information on 'significant discrepancies' between attainments in assessments and National Curriculum core subject tests and the attainment of the majority of the peer group. Also there should be a discrepancy in what the pupil actually achieves in the above assessments and what others, teachers and parents/carers, feel could be achieved. This should be supported by standardised tests 'as can reliably be administered'. The third discrepancy is within and between the core subjects of the National Curriculum. This set of criteria is similar to those set out in the previous Code. An addition has been made for children in the early years, discrepancies in their attainments of the early learning goals compared with peer attainment.

What the present document has achieved is to stop the repetitive sections of the former Code. However, because of the general nature now presented schools may have to look very carefully at individual pupils to determine whether after being supported at School Action Plus a Statement would be the only option.

The LEA has to weigh up the documentation provided and look at the above evidence on attainment, the other factors pertaining to specific learning difficulties which have been mentioned previously in this book and decide whether the evidence 'points to under-attainment rather than special educational needs'. The LEA also has to look at the provision provided, set out in paragraphs 7:46–7:54, and tried by the school in order to determine whether the child's learning difficulties 'have not responded to relevant and purposeful measures taken by the school and external specialists' and so these 'may call for special educational provision which cannot reasonably be provided within the resources normally available to mainstream schools in the area'.

Again the points, such as those in paragraph 7:49, are general to all special educational needs but within these are statements that are relevant to any action made by the school for pupils with specific learning difficulties. These range from monitoring and evaluating the IEPs to measuring progress by different forms of assessment. Both the views of the parents/carers and the pupil should have been sought. External guidance should have been requested if the pupil showed signs of social, emotional and behavioural difficulties. Pertinent to specific learning difficulties are the two points that cover literacy support. It is suggested that schools should have used 'structured reading and spelling programmes, and multi-sensory teaching strategies to enhance the National Literacy ... Framework(s)' and that appropriate information technology has been accessed which includes word processing with spell checkers.

There are a great many hurdles to jump over before a statutory assessment is initiated and LEAs will have their own additional criteria and basis for who should qualify for a Statement. The balance of evidence presented has to show that the child's specific learning difficulties are significant and/or complex and ideas on this will differ from LEA to LEA. LEAs will also differ in their level of special educational needs resourcing for schools so how Statements will be allocated will be different from area to area. There is a section about this in the Code, chapter 8.

School Action requires schools to begin to take 'additional or different' action by using their existing resources whereas School Action Plus allocates extra resources from the LEA. Sometimes this will be through the provision of a Statement of Special Educational Needs; sometimes there will be extra delegated resources, either monetary or from external agency support, so a Statement will not be necessary. Section 7 in the *SEN Toolkit* is titled 'Writing a Statement of Special Educational Needs'. It states that LEAs should be specific when determining the provision required and that usually this should be quantified in both hours and frequency of support. However, it shows that schools can retain some flexibility where provision is concerned and provides some examples of this in para. 37. One of the examples is for pupils with severe specific learning difficulties, although the term 'severe' is not defined. However, this guidance accepts that such pupils may have variations in the way they perform in and access different curriculum areas and how their significant literacy difficulties might impede this access. Thus they might require some 'targeted' 1:1 support which, in mainstream education, will probably be teaching assistant support but it could also be teacher-based. It also could take place within a group situation. The example suggests that this support might be helping with multi-sensory reading and spelling programmes plus support in other curriculum areas where literacy is a problem. Although the provision itself should be detailed on the Statement the level and nature of the support could be left for the school to organise.

As with the previous Code it is suggested that LEAs set up a moderating group (para. 8:9), in order to ensure that the evidence received from schools leads to consistent administration of which pupils are allocated a Statement of Special Educational Needs. They may wish to determine whether the child's learning difficulties have been well assessed and that the child's special educational provision is appropriate or whether the LEA can give extra advice and support through School Action Plus. They may also require certain LEA staff to monitor those pupils with a Statement of Special Educational Needs to determine whether the allocated resources are being used effectively.

LEAs may determine additional criteria for ceasing to maintain a Statement. This procedure might be suggested by the school and agreed to by the parents/carers when the child no longer requires additional support and resources and can access the curriculum with relative ease. Or the LEA may set guidelines where LEA staff monitor and review a child's progress and when the child reaches a certain literacy level and has appropriate coping strategies there may be no further need for the Statement to be maintained. It would be hoped that all former aspects of the pupil's difficulties would be reassessed rather than basing the criteria for destatementing on a single educational aspect, such as reading competency. The Code sets out some criteria for ceasing to maintain the Statement in paragraphs 8:117–8:124.

An example of what might be written on a Statement
Part 2 describes the pupil's special educational needs with a short general descriptive account and some statements to identify the learning difficulties. (Quotations from the actual Statement are set in italics.)

Kevin is described as a boy with specific learning difficulties in terms of developing basic skills. He has poor auditory short-term memory skills and a poor visual memory which gives him problems in retaining sight words without constant reinforcement. Recent tests have indicated that Kevin functions intellectually at an average level and he is said to be quite creative. Kevin is also described as becoming increasingly withdrawn at school and his self-esteem is said to be low. The LEA has identified Kevin's learning difficulties as follows:

1. poor auditory short-term memory skills which inhibit his ability to acquire basic literacy through a phonic approach;

2. weak visual memory skills which inhibit his ability to acquire literacy skills through visual channels;

3. low self-confidence and self-esteem.

Part 3 which specifies the Special Educational Provision is in three parts which state the objectives, the educational provision to meet needs and objectives, and monitoring arrangements.

The objectives translate the stated learning difficulties into long-term aims.

1. to acquire a more complete and reliable phonic knowledge so as to develop his ability to read for information and enjoyment;

2. to develop and extend his sight vocabulary so as to help him become more accurate at reading;

3. to develop and extend his spelling skills so as to extend his ability to communicate effectively in writing;

4. to promote his confidence and enhance his self-esteem.

The provision states what the school should provide with LEA support if this is specified. In Kevin's case this was an additional two hours' teaching support in order to carry out an intense, structured literacy programme. The provision section may also say that the advisory teachers should be consulted where necessary. The monitoring section sets out that the Individual Education Plan should be drawn up with appropriate short-term educational targets within two months of receiving the final Statement and should be sent to the parents and to the LEA. Monitoring and Annual Reviews have to be carried out.

Whole School Policy

Chapter 1 of the Code of Practice (2001) covers 'Principles and Policies'. In this chapter the duties of the governing bodies are stated and one of these is publicising the school policy on special educational needs. There is information about what should be contained in the SEN policy in Annex A.

The parts of this that are particularly applicable to this publication are statements 5, 8, 13, 14 and 17. Statement 5 requires information on the kinds of special educational needs provision in which the school specialises and any special units it organises. There are mainstream schools that provide small units, either part-time or full-time, for pupils with specific learning difficulties. These either are an added facility for the particular school or a resource within the LEA. It is also becoming more common to find members of staff in schools having some extra qualification for the teaching of specific learning difficulties (e.g. OCR diploma/DI diploma/advanced diploma from universities) and it is important that use is made of this knowledge for the benefit of both pupils and other staff members.

Statement 8 asks for information about how pupils with special educational needs are identified, how their needs are determined and then reviewed. Schools should be able to present evidence that they are aware that there is a difference between specific and general learning difficulties which they are assessing through appropriate techniques and should be making suitable arrangements for teaching, monitoring and reviewing. (This is dealt with in Chapters 2, 3 and 4.)

Arrangements made by the governing body relating to in-service training for staff in relation to special educational needs are covered in statement 13. If schools are to recognise and accept that specific learning difficulties are a separate section within the realm of special educational needs then staff as a whole need to be aware of the problems experienced by such pupils. Also if individual members of staff want to acquire further specialist knowledge about specific learning difficulties they should be encouraged to undertake this and funding should be made available.

Statement 14 refers to the use made of teachers and facilities from outside the school including support services for special educational needs. LEAs differ in their provision of psychological services and support and advisory services but where there are LEAs providing particular 'experts' for specific learning difficulties these should be mentioned with reference to how they are consulted and used.

Reference to links with any voluntary organisations that work on behalf of children with special educational needs is in statement 17. There are voluntary bodies such as local Dyslexia Associations with whom schools may have contact. There may be a member of staff who is a member of such a body and, where possible, relevant literature received should be shared.

Specific learning difficulties can be subsumed within the other parts of the policy where provision, access to the curriculum, integration and parental partnership are concerned.

Resourcing special educational needs comes from the school's budget. Some LEAs work out formulae for providing extra funding for those schools whose percentage of children with special educational needs are deemed to be greater than would be normally expected. Specific learning difficulties resourcing needs will have to be measured from within the overall budget and there will be organisational implications for dealing with individuals' problems. Examples of practice are given in the previous chapter 'Classroom strategies at School Action and School Action Plus' which will show how both group and individual work can be carried out.

It is believed that about 20% of children nationally may have some form of special educational need at some time in their school life and about 18% of these will have their needs met in their mainstream schools. This leaves about 2% for whom a statutory Statement of Special Educational Need may be necessary. It should be kept in mind that most of this remaining 2% will be in specialised schooling. Of course percentages will vary over LEAs and schools. Since the Code of Practice (1994) this percentage rose considerably in many LEAs. The earlier Code used figures in paragraph 2:2 to indicate the proportion of children requiring to have their special educational needs met within the educational system but the Code of Practice (2001) refrains from this practice.

As it has been stated in the introduction, the British Dyslexia Association gives percentages for those pupils suffering from specific learning difficulties which are 4% having severe problems (or as they say about one in every class) and up to 10% having some type of specific learning difficulty that would need attention.

Staff Development

It has been mentioned earlier that in-service training of staff should feature on the school's special educational needs policy. This often becomes one of the responsibilities of the SENCO (see below). It is important to point out that in-service training should cover the needs of both teachers and teaching assistants.

73

The SENCO

The Code of Practice (2001) outlines the role of SENCO in the three stages of education. In mainstream primary and secondary schools the key responsibilities may include:

- being responsible for the day-by-day execution of the school's special educational needs policy;

- co-ordinating the provision for pupils with special educational needs;

- working with other members of staff (liaison and advice);

- managing teaching assistants;

- overseeing the records (which would include IEPs) of those pupils who have been identified as having special educational needs;

- liaising with parents/carers of pupils with special educational needs;

- contributing to staff in-service training;

- working with external agencies (the LEA's support and pyschological services, health and social services and voluntary bodies).
(Adapted from para 5:32)

The only difference for the secondary sector (para. 6:35) is that other key responsibilities are:

- managing the special educational needs team (teachers and teaching assistants);

- the addition of working with the Connexions PA to the list of external agencies.

Therefore, if the school is going to require the SENCO for in-school staff development before this occurs, he or she may have to be provided with some extra training. Some co-ordinators may have general additional qualifications in special educational needs or may be equipped with a particular specialism but this might not cover specific learning difficulties. There are national courses in this particular area of special need which could be taken up. Some of these lead to further qualifications and some are of a shorter duration. Often these are organised by the OCR, British Dyslexia Association, the Dyslexia Institute or the Helen Arkell Centre or by education departments attached to universities. However, not all SENCOs would be able to undertake such training either because of the financial aspect or because of the travel and/or boarding implications. LEAs should mount courses for SENCOs dealing with the specific learning difficulties so that these staff members are:

- able to recognise the differences between a child with specific learning difficulties and one with general learning difficulties;

- aware of the additional problems children with specific learning difficulties may face (e.g. dyslexia, dyspraxia, dysgraphia, dyscalculia, dysphasia);

- able to use appropriate identification and assessment procedures;

- able to advise on differentiated techniques within the classroom;

- knowledgeable about the materials available;

- knowledgeable about the teaching programmes available both for groups and individuals;

- able to advise on and write IEPs for School Action and School Action Plus which can be monitored;

- confident in deciding which pupils can work within School Action, School Action Plus and which ones may require a Statement;

- able to liaise with parents/carers and formulate partnership approaches;

- able to co-ordinate all the relevant information required if a pupil is felt to need a statutory assessment;

- able to transfer the requirements of the Statement onto an IEP;

- able to provide in-service training for the staff of their particular school.

Courses such as these should preferably lead to some kind of certification either from the LEA or validated from a college of higher education. They should be run by LEA staff who have appropriate qualifications or skills or by external specialists. It is not reasonable to expect SENCOs to undertake detailed courses such as these in twilight sessions. If LEAs are to recognise the needs of pupils with specific learning difficulties then release cover should be made available and SENCOs directed to attend. It may not be realistic for a SENCO from every school to be expected to attend such a course since schools differ in size, especially those in the primary sector. It may be more relevant, therefore, to have courses such as the above mounted for the secondary SENCOs and one primary SENCO in a pyramid or cluster of schools. Then the training can be given to the other primary SENCOs in a less 'formal' situation or as a rolling programme over the years.

If SENCOs have no additional expertise and/or training in special educational needs in general, these teachers should have a thorough knowledge of the processes of literacy development. Sessions for this should cover:

- the development and teaching of speaking and listening and how these influence the process of reading;

- the development of reading which would include:
  - phonological awareness and the auditory skills
  - visual skills
  - word attack skills (including phonics, sight words and context)
  - multi-sensory approaches
  - higher reading skills
  - appraisal of published material
  - readability
  - assessment (including miscue analysis, sub-skills, standardised tests);

- the development of spelling which would include:
  - auditory and visual processes
  - spelling stages
  - strategies for teaching spelling
  - appraisal of published material
  - assessment (including miscue analysis, sub-skills, standardised tests);

- the development of written work which would include:
  - handwriting (including letter formation, legibility and flow, posture and pen hold and handedness)
  - emergent writing
  - higher writing skills.

It would be helpful if additional information was given about numeracy problems and the acquisition of mathematical concepts and processes. Also it is important for teachers to know about learning styles and strategies for children to cope with their specific learning problems.

In paragraphs 5:35–5:36 and 6:36–6:40 the Code suggests that because of the responsibilities of the SENCO this position requires time for planning and co-ordination, the maintenance of the paperwork, the management of learning support assistants and liaison with colleagues within the school and other educational establishments. It also recommends that it is helpful if the SENCO has access to a telephone, is supported by relevant Information and Communication Technology (ICT) and has a suitable room for interviewing. It is pointed out that the role of SENCO is comparable to other major co-ordinator roles, in the case of secondary schools, being equivalent to heads of department or heads of year. If SENCOs have sufficient time and support for their role then all pupils with special educational needs, including those with specific learning difficulties, will benefit.

The special needs department staff
The type of information and training needed for other members of staff would be different from that given to the co-ordinators although there would be some similarities. Members of special needs departments would need information on:

- the differences between a child with specific learning difficulties and one with general learning difficulties;

- the use of appropriate identification and assessment procedures;

- the materials available;

- how to write IEPs for School Action, both individual and group plans, and how to monitor IEPs in School Action and School Action Plus;

- the delivery of particular learning programmes.

This information could be disseminated in special needs department meetings either in their own school or with other support teachers in other schools. LEA advisory teachers could be called in to help with running the sessions if this is deemed necessary.

Support teachers and those working with children with literacy problems also need more generalised knowledge about literacy (and maybe numeracy) as outlined in the section for SENCOs.

Class and subject teachers

Class and subject teachers should be given information about specific learning difficulties at least once a year. This could be given at a staff meeting and should be the responsibility of the SENCO. It is also advisable to update staff about actual individuals' problems. Where secondary staff are concerned it may be advisable to also give them a profile of individual children (see the appendix 1 for an example). Also in secondary schools it is sometimes easier for the SENCO to attend departmental meetings in order to focus on the particular concerns of that curriculum area. Some secondary schools appoint 'link' members of staff from curriculum areas who meet regularly with the special needs department. Staff should be told about:

- the differences between a child with specific learning difficulties and one with general learning difficulties and be aware of the problems he or she may have in accessing the curriculum;

- how to organise differentiated techniques within the classroom;

- any materials available for helping children with specific learning difficulties within their classrooms;

- the use of IEPs for School Action and School Action Plus and how these should be monitored.

Learning support assistants/teaching assistants

Some schools require support assistants to undertake both supporting and teaching roles. Therefore, not only do these members of the school staff need to attend the staff meetings but they may also require some specialised in-service training. They need to be made aware of why they are carrying out a particular teaching programme and how they should record results. Many LEAs organise generalised courses for non-teaching assistants and very often these refer in particular to literacy and behavioural aspects. However, non-teaching assistants also need to understand the differences in learning approaches of the child with specific learning difficulties and the child with general learning difficulties. They also need some basic information about the processes of reading and spelling and why particular methods are used in teaching these literacy areas.

Governors

Governors also have in-service needs because of their duties where special educational needs are concerned (see the Code of Practice 1:16). If the school's policy is going to include particular sections about specific learning difficulties then the governors, in particular if there is a governor who has been given responsibility for special educational needs and who may be the 'responsible person', should be aware of the different categories of special educational need which include specific learning difficulties. Often LEAs put special educational needs as an item for governors' training and within that there should be time allotted for a definition and explanation of specific learning difficulties.

The LEA

Most schools work within the framework of an LEA and these local education authorities have different ways of meeting the needs of pupils with specific learning difficulties. There may be support teams of peripatetic teachers who work with children with literacy difficulties. Some authorities employ teachers who have specialist qualifications for specific learning difficulties who undertake in-school teaching programmes. Some authorities have specialist advisory teachers who assess and monitor children with difficulties at the more severe end of the specific learning difficulties continuum. There are, in some LEAs, specialist centres which work on a tutorial basis for literacy support while others provide special classes where pupils have intensive literacy help alongside other areas of the curriculum either within the class or in the mainstream of the host school.

Schools that have been given grant-maintained status may also be able to use the services provided by their LEA by purchasing the support. These schools can also call upon other LEA teams or independent teams for advice.

Independent schools

If a pupil has very severe specific learning difficulties and it is deemed that he or she will take a long time to learn to acquire the processes for competent reading or has attendant emotional/behavioural problems which are impeding learning then some LEAs will fund day or residential placement in the independent school sector.

Parents/Carers and Pupils

Working with parents/carers

The concept of parental partnership with schools was enshrined in the Code of Practice (1994), sections 2:28–2:33, and parents/carers' involvement in their child's education was given emphasis throughout the school's staged processes and this was carried on into the area of statutory assessment if appropriate.

> *'Children's progress will be diminished if their parents are not seen as partners in the educational process with unique knowledge and information to impart. Professional help can seldom be wholly effective unless it builds upon parents' capacity to be involved and unless parents consider that professionals take account of what they say and treat their views and anxieties as intrinsically important.'*
>
> (DfEE, 1994, para. 2:28)

The importance of working with parents/carers has continued within the *SEN Code of Practice* (2001) and in its introduction it states:

> *'Parents hold key information and have a critical role to play in their children's education. There are strong reasons for working in partnership with all parents. If they feel confident that schools and professionals actively involve them, take account of their wishes, feelings and unique perspectives on their children's development, then the work of those schools and professionals can be more effective. This is particularly so, if a child has special needs. All parents of children with special educational needs should feel they are treated as partners...'*
>
> (para. 2:2)

This paragraph continues by stating that parents should feel 'able and empowered' to contribute an active role in their child's education which would be felt to be of merit. They should feel that any problems their child might have would be identified at an early stage of education and appropriate intervention strategies would be given; that they should have a meaningful say in their child's education and that they should be kept informed at all stages.

Section 2: Parent Partnership Services in the *SEN Toolkit* is a helpful document which should be read in connection with Chapter 2 in the Code.

LEAs are required to arrange for parents/carers to be given information and advice on their child's special educational needs and usually this is done through parent partnership services which carry out a full range of services. One of these is to make sure that parents/carers can be supported by an Independent Parental Supporter (IPS), someone who is independent of those within the education service, if they so wish.

LEAs also have to provide disagreement resolution services for those cases where parents/carers might disagree with the school over any aspects of special educational needs provision. This service should be seen to be one that is independent in nature and also one that works towards informal solutions. Parents/carers may still have the right to apply to the SEN Tribunal but it is hoped that the disagreement resolution services would negate this need. Chapter 2 in the Code, paragraphs 2:22–2:30, give details of this.

Parents/carers may be the initiators of the staged process. If they have any concerns or if there is anxiety felt about their child having a specific learning difficulty schools should treat these with concern and give them due attention. Parents/carers should be given information about specific learning difficulties in understandable terms. Some may have already sought out such information from voluntary associations, have read articles from magazines and/or newspapers, have listened to radio programmes or have watched TV programmes. They may obtain mixed messages. Schools might feel that the child's specific learning problem is mild and can be helped by differentiated in-class support whereas outside independent advice has mentioned the necessity for statutory assessment leading to a Statement. Schools must be wary of labelling parents/carers as over-anxious or 'pushy' as by doing so they may tend to disregard the concern. Parents/carers want the best for their children and, therefore, it would be helpful if their worries were either talked through or they were given generalised information such as:

Explanation of specific learning difficulties and other learning problems

- Some children find the process of reading and spelling very difficult. They may have no problems with other subjects and seem to be better at answering than coping with the written word. If these children have specific learning difficulties then they learn to read and spell in different ways from the other children in their class.

- Some children have learning difficulties because they have missed a lot of schooling. Some may have had health problems or sensory problems such as 'glue ear' which have hindered their rate of learning. Some children may have changed schools a lot and may have been taught by different methods. Some children are generally slower and will learn everything at a slower pace.

- There are no 'cures' as such for children with specific learning difficulties. However, given appropriate teaching the difficulties may lessen. Often reading improves but spelling may remain a long-term problem.

- Not all children with specific learning difficulties have the same problems. Some have mild problems and can be helped within the ordinary classroom. Some have more serious and long-term problems so may have to be assessed by an advisory teacher and/or educational psychologist. These children may be given special teaching programmes.

Identification of a child with specific learning difficulties
Specific learning difficulties may be detected if the child:

- fails to make the expected progress in reading and spelling even though there seems to be no reason for this;

- shows uneven performance in school subjects especially where progress is seen in those subjects and those areas that do not require spelling and reading performance;

- is taking a long time to develop the skills of learning to read and to write;

- shows there are problems with visual memory so that it is hard to remember words by sight for both reading and spelling;

- shows there are problems with auditory memory so that it is hard to use sounds for reading and spelling. There are also problems with saying rhymes and giving rhyming words;

- shows there are organisational and general memory problems so that the child finds it difficult to remember things like messages.

What the school might undertake if a child has specific learning difficulties

- If specific learning difficulties are suspected then the school will try different types of teaching.

- There are school-based stages, School Action and School Action Plus, which can be put into operation.

- There are particular programmes of work which can be put into operation in order to help the child.

- The 'special arrangements' procedures for tests and examinations can be requested and put into practice.

What the LEA might undertake if the child's specific learning difficulties are deemed severe

- The roles of any LEA 'specialist' should be explained.

- The criteria for making a request for statutory assessment and the LEA procedures for dealing with this should be gone through.

- The benefits of a Statement should be identified.

- Access to an Independent Parental Supporter should be given, if required.

Parental assistance for a child with specific learning difficulties

- Sometimes specific learning difficulties run in families so there may be someone else with a similar problem.

- Families can help a child who has specific learning difficulties by:
  - being patient when the child has problems remembering
  - being supportive and helpful in trying to help the child organise his or her day
  - making sure that other members of the family do not laugh at the child's mistakes or label him or her 'thick' or 'stupid'. If the child loses confidence learning becomes more difficult.

- Families can help to teach the child with specific learning difficulties but it depends on the particular child and the family. Some children find it hard to see their parents/carers as teachers. Some parents/carers find it hard to take on the teacher role especially because they have to keep very patient and encouraging. Very close liaison should take place with the school and the teachers. Parents/carers should try to undertake things as the school would do, so good home-school information is needed.

Pointers like this can be talked through with both the parents/carers and the teacher making factual statements about the child which fit with any particular detail that is raised. Parents/carers should be able to add other observations and the teacher can show evidence of the child's performance from classwork and National Curriculum attainments. If it is felt that the child should be placed on School Action then this should happen with a built-in review date so that the parent/carer knows when the next meeting will be.

In order to help children with specific learning difficulties to consolidate their learning in school it is important that they work with their parents/carers at home. There will be some families who will not be able to cope here and these families should not be penalised by the school. Parents/carers will have to be given direct instructions as to what to do with particular programmes but in general the following suggestions for parents/carers can be given:

- Be positive.

- Be patient.

- Praise and encourage.

- Try to avoid failure and stress situations.

- Listen to the child's problems and try to understand them.

- Keep a sense of humour.

- Know when to change the activity.

- Do not compete with a favourite television programme or other activity.

- Work with the child individually if other siblings distract or are more able.

- Share your observations with the school.

- Help with organisational problems.

- Help with but do not 'do' homework.

- Encourage regular practice in problem areas.

It would be more helpful for all concerned if parents/carers could learn to recognise and accept their child as being 'learning different' rather than having a 'deficit' in his or her learning. A specific learning difficulty, unlike an illness, cannot be readily 'cured'. But it can be helped by teaching to the child's strengths and alongside this working to overcome the weaknesses. Strategies can be given to enable the child to access the curriculum areas and to help any of his or her particular organisational problems. Positive support rather than expressions of concern will foster strong and clear feelings of self-worth in the child. If children are to cope with difficulties, wherever they are on the continuum of specific learning difficulties, they will need both encouragement and acceptance especially from their immediate families.

Working with pupils
The *SEN Code of Practice* (2001) has a chapter devoted to Pupil Participation where the rights of the child to make informed decisions about the education received and to be aware of why certain things have been put in place are specified.

'All children should be involved in making decisions right from the start. The ways in which children are encouraged to participate should develop to reflect the child's evolving maturity. Participation in education is a process that will necessitate all children being given the opportunity to make choices and to understand that their views matter.'

(para. 3:6)

It is suggested that pupils, as far as they are able, should take part in the decision-making processes that determine their education. They should be involved in the assessment and review of their particular special needs. They should contribute to the setting of their learning targets and how these form their IEPs. If they are given a Statement of Special Educational Needs then they should attend review meetings and this is particularly relevant when their Transition Plan is prepared. Section 4: Enabling Pupil Participation in the *SEN Toolkit* contains many general suggestions which cover, among other areas, whole school approaches and how pupils with varying special needs can be helped to take part in decision-making about their own learning requirements. Many pupils with specific learning difficulties are articulate and well able to voice opinions and bring suggestions which might strengthen the way they learn.

Often pupils with specific learning difficulties move on to colleges of further or higher education and, as with earlier transfers between primary and secondary establishments, they can find this a daunting prospect. If they have a Statement of Special Educational Need this transfer might be made easier because of the specific meeting that is held where problem areas can be discussed. However, the majority of pupils with specific learning difficulties will not have Statements but they still require support if they are going to choose the most appropriate course for them and the further education establishment that is best suited for someone with their particular level of difficulty.

Conclusion

The ultimate aim for parents/carers, teachers, school and the LEA is that the support given to and the programme provided for any particular child with specific learning difficulties will show success. Correct assessment and correct ways of meeting needs can show progress. Each pupil has to be assessed on an individual basis and his or her needs met in the best way possible, whether this is within the school or with the additional help of a Statement or in rarer cases in other types of school. No one solution meets every case.

An example to show the progress that may be made since first identification was made

Concern was felt about Joe's literacy problems when he was 5 years 8 months old and he was referred to the Advisory Teacher for Learning Support at 6 years 6 months who found the following:

- He lacked confidence and although articulate was very quiet in class.

- His receptive language abilities were very high.

- His poor short-term visual memory meant that he could recall six keywords and a few other words from the reading scheme books. He would only write four words independently.

- He had visual directional and sequencing problems.

- He had poor phonological problems (unable to rhyme and cope with whispered blendings) although he could hear initial sounds and write some.

- His handwriting was very poor.

- He had organisational problems.

Programmes of work were suggested and carried out. At 8 years 2 months he was seen by an LEA educational psychologist and his IQ was measured as above average. At 9 years 3 months he was given a Statement of Special Educational Needs and two hours' teaching was set up as well as the in-school support.

At 10 years 7 months the Advisory Teacher for Specific Learning Difficulties reviewed his progress and found:

- He was very confident and pleased about his progress and he took part in all classroom activities.

- He sight read with ease 196/200 keywords.

- His NRA A reading accuracy midpoint was 7.6 years and he used context and phonic decoding skills.

- He had worked through a phonic programme up to vowel digraphs.

- His spelling age measured at 7.2 years on Schonell Spelling Test and his attempts at unknown words showed that he could use quite reasonable sound letter patterns. He could write a great deal of work that would communicate with the reader.

His continued problems were self-organisation and directional problems. The programme would continue into the secondary sector until his reading became at least at a functional level where he was felt to be able to access the separate subject areas.

All children have individual needs of some kind. Children with specific learning difficulties have very particular individual needs. Specific learning difficulties should not be considered a 'handicapping condition' but rather as something that should be recognised as distinct to the individual which requires description and attention. These children are 'learning different'. The majority of children with specific learning difficulties can be helped within school without the support of a statement of Special Educational Needs at School Action or School Action Plus.

The first important factor is the individual's self-esteem, his or her acceptance and understanding of the problem and his or her ability to be positive when the 'going seems tough'. The second important factor is the understanding of others, both peers, family and teachers, so that everyone works with the individual to help him or her to either overcome the specific problems or to find strategies of working round them.

Owen, a 13-year-old boy of average intelligence with no measurable reading and spelling skills, declared 'it's the same principle' (meaning that the label he had been given of specific learning difficulties meant the same thing as unintelligence). Because of this perspective he gave up on learning. A counterpart with similar intelligence and attainment levels, Michael, accessed his way into the mainstream curriculum with the words 'I'll have to do it my way.'

Teachers who care will want to help change any such negative views shown by pupils. And they will.

Appendices

Appendix 1
A Basic Information Check-Sheet for Secondary Schools

The following can form a basic information sheet which can be given as it stands to secondary school members of staff. It will serve to give them some global factors about the problems experienced by pupils with specific learning difficulties and to give some hints about how to deal with such problems. However, lists such as these can be personalised so two examples are also given.

INFORMATION FOR SUBJECT TEACHERS

If you teach a pupil with specific learning difficulties he or she may:

- have problems with the mechanical side to reading although understanding the content;

- be well able to cope orally;

- have problems with spelling. This can show in these respects:
  1) only simple words are written to avoid errors
  2) words are readable but incorrect
  3) words are unreadable;

- have poor numeracy skills;

- have problems with handwriting. Often poor handwriting is adopted to mask spelling errors;

- have problems with written work because of poor study skills;

- have problems with taking notes from dictation or copying notes from the board;

- have problems with following instructions;

- produce limited written work and homework;

- have low self-esteem and lack of confidence;

- be a slow worker because of difficulties;

- lack concentration;

- have organisational problems;

- become tired because of the concentration needed and, therefore, become inconsistent in performance.

It would be helpful if you would:

GENERALLY

- Praise and encourage and find something he or she is good at.

- Let him or her sit where you can help without doing so obtrusively.

- Encourage oral responses.

- Not always expect as much classwork or homework as from others.

- Try and vary the activities and break up sustained activities into smaller ones (small tasks).

- Use appropriate language both when talking and presenting written work.

- Use the computer if appropriate.

- Make work achievable.

- Examine your methods of assessment and maybe modify these.

- Involve parents/carers and keep them informed of progress and problems.

- Use parents/carers' help where appropriate.

- Use the blackboard as little as possible.

WHERE READING IS CONCERNED

- Do not insist on reading aloud if he or she finds this a problem.

- Help with unfamiliar subject words.

- Liaise with the special needs department or learning support advisory staff to help teach unfamiliar words or go through work to be read.

- Help with study skills (e.g. skimming/scanning/main points etc.).

- Keep your own handwriting legible to facilitate pupils' reading.

WHERE SPELLING IS CONCERNED

- Mark written work on content not spelling to encourage use of a wide vocabulary.

- Only correct a few errors.

- Teach necessary subject words – but do not overload.

- Liaise with the special needs department or learning support advisory staff to help teach necessary words.

- Allow him or her to read back the work if words are unreadable.

- Do not expect dictionary work as this may be too difficult to be used.

WHERE WRITTEN WORK IS CONCERNED

- Encourage him or her to smarten up handwriting but do not expect it to be changed.

- Do not ask him or her to write out work again unless he or she has not taken any care.

- Either give more time or allow another pupil to make a carbon copy if note-taking is difficult.

- Give less written work.

A personalised information sheet for a pupil transferring to the secondary sector on a Stage 2 (which would be School Action)

INFORMATION FOR SUBJECT TEACHERS

GERMAINE _____ d.o.b. _____
_____ HIGH

Germaine has some specific learning difficulties which have affected his reading and spelling skills. He is on a Record of Support Stage 2. He also suffers from light sensitivity (Scotopic Sensitivity Syndrome) and uses overlays to read through. Germaine can read texts around the 10 years readability level but his understanding is better than his oral reading. He should be able to cope with most of the texts given in the subject areas. He finds small, closely packed print a problem. His written work communicates rather than containing totally accurate spellings. Germaine may find it difficult to copy notes from the board.

It would be helpful if you would:

GENERALLY

- Be aware of his SSS problems and that he is unable to use his overlays for any work other than reading texts.

WHERE READING IS CONCERNED

- Do not insist on oral reading if he finds this a problem.

- Help with unfamiliar subject words.

- Help with study skills (e.g. skimming/scanning/main points etc.).

- Keep your own handwriting legible to facilitate his reading.

WHERE SPELLING IS CONCERNED

- Mark written work on content not spelling to encourage use of a wide vocabulary.

- Only correct a few errors.

- Teach necessary subject words – but do not overload.

- Liaise with the special needs department or learning support advisory staff to help teach necessary words.

WHERE WRITTEN WORK IS CONCERNED

- Either give more time or allow another pupil to make a carbon copy if note-taking is difficult.

A personalised information sheet for a pupil transferring to the secondary sector with a Statement of Special Educational Needs.

INFORMATION FOR SUBJECT TEACHERS

ALEX _____ d.o.b. _____
_____ HIGH

Alex has specific learning difficulties which mean that his reading and spelling attainments do not match his general abilities. He is an intelligent pupil. He has a Statement of Special Educational Needs. Alex can read texts around the 7 year readability level and his written work is weak and there may be times when his spellings do not communicate. Alex will find it difficult to take notes from dictation or copy notes from the board and he may have difficulties with following instructions. It is possible that he will produce less written work and homework than his peers. Alex has quite good self-esteem but this took a long time to build up so it is felt that his present self-confidence is fragile. He has some speech and articulation problems.

It would be helpful if you would:

GENERALLY

- Praise and encourage and find something he is good at.

- Let him sit where you can help without doing so obtrusively.

- Encourage oral responses.

- Not always expect as much classwork or homework as from others.

- Use appropriate language both when talking and presenting written work.

- Make work achievable.

- Examine your methods of assessment and maybe modify these.

- Use the blackboard as little as possible.

WHERE READING IS CONCERNED

- Do not insist on oral reading as he will find this a problem.

- Help with unfamiliar subject words.

- Liaise with the special needs department or learning support advisory staff to help teach unfamiliar words or go through work to be read.

- Keep your own handwriting legible to facilitate his reading.

WHERE SPELLING IS CONCERNED

- Mark written work on content not spelling to encourage use of a wide vocabulary.

- Only correct a few errors.

- Teach necessary subject words – but do not overload.

- Liaise with the special needs department or learning support advisory staff to help teach necessary words.

- Allow him to read back the work if words are unreadable.

- Do not expect dictionary work as this may be too difficult to be used.

WHERE WRITTEN WORK IS CONCERNED

- Encourage him to smarten up handwriting but do not expect it to be changed.

- Do not ask him to write out work again unless he has not taken any care.

- Either give more time or allow another pupil to make a carbon copy if note-taking is difficult.

- Give less written work.

- Allow alternatives for recording if it is felt that he cannot get his thoughts down on paper.

Appendix 2
Some Definitions of Other Specific Learning Difficulties

Dyslexia
Dr Chris Singleton gives two definitions when lecturing on the subject. In simple terms he states it is 'an unexpected difficulty in acquiring effective literacy skills'. Early definitions of dyslexia were concerned solely with reading attainment and only in more recent years has dyslexia broadened to take in other areas of learning. However, because this rather uncomplicated statement does not seem to give the full picture Dr Singleton has amplified it. The definition then states that 'Developmental dyslexia is a constitutional condition which results in differences in some aspects of information processing by the brain and which causes difficulties in specific areas of learning, particularly literacy skills.' He specifies that it is helpful to think of differences rather than deficits for a difference in the way an individual learns should lead to a difference in the way he or she is taught.

Dyspraxia

Dyspraxia is also a probable constitutional condition where the dyspraxic individual has problems with learning and acquiring patterns of movement. It is a dysfunction of co-ordination and shows itself in poor spatial awareness, problems with handwriting and gross and fine motor control. For some children there are co-ordination problems with the muscles which co-ordinate the movement needed for speech. Therefore, some children have verbal and/or articulatory dyspraxia where they find it difficult to speak clearly and to express themselves efficiently. Speech therapists and occupational therapists may become involved with children whose dyspraxia is quite severe.

Dysgraphia

Because of the problems that some individuals were found to have with graphomotor (handwriting) skills and other fine motor skills (such as using scissors, tying laces) the term 'dysgraphia' was employed as another sub-set of the specific learning difficulties family. However, 'dyspraxia' seems to be the term more commonly used today showing that terminology can alter over the years.

Dysphasia

This is a specific problem of language rather than of articulation problems. Language difficulties can either be receptive or expressive or a mixture of both. Receptive language is concerned with the understanding of words and how they are used. Expressive language is concerned with how one uses words to convey meaning. A specialised speech and language assessment is usually needed in order to gain the knowledge necessary for identification and remediation of severe language problems. However, there are certain language behaviours that can alert teachers and parents/carers to a particular problem especially if these persist past the age when they are acceptable.

Dyscalculia

This term means that an individual has a particular specific problem in the area of numeracy. Some children seem to have solely this one 'block' within their learning capabilities. Many others who have specific learning difficulties in acquiring literacy skills also have similar problems with number. Problems with short and long-term memories, directional confusion, sequencing and perceptual difficulties and problems with spatial awareness can make learning number sequences, tables, place value etc.

96

extremely difficult. Added to these can come the more generalised problems pertaining to mathematics such as the language of mathematics and mathematical problem solving. It is felt by many that there is less of a stigma in being termed 'innumerate' rather than being termed 'illiterate' and that individuals can cope in life with poorly developed numeracy skills.

Appendix 3
Other 'Companions' to the
Specific Learning Difficulties Range

Scotopic Sensitivity Syndrome (SSS) or Irlen Syndrome

This can be termed a condition that is often found alongside other learning difficulties rather than a learning difficulty in itself. Its origin is from America where Helen Irlen first discovered that certain individuals found it easier to read through coloured overlays. SSS is a perceptual dysfunction not a problem of actual eyesight and screeners always recommend that a thorough eyesight examination is undertaken if SSS problems are suspected and later detected. For some individuals it seems that the brain has difficulties with processing information from full spectral light. It is not a condition just experienced by those with specific learning difficulties but many pupils with specific literacy problems particularly in the visual field may also have SSS. Research continues to be carried out into the reasons why some individuals suffer from this syndrome.

There are a range of problems that can be experienced by individuals who are said to have SSS. These are:

- light sensitivity:
  where individuals find it a problem working under strong sunlight or fluorescent lighting;

- black-white contrast:
  where individuals find it difficult to cope with the black print on bright white pages;

- print distortion:
  where individuals find that letters on the page move or even disappear;

- span of recognition:
  where difficulties occur with keeping on track on the page when reading;

- concentration and attention:
  where individuals become very sleepy or restless when having to stay on task during reading and writing activities;

- distance and spatial relationship problems:
  where there are difficulties with judging differences in distance, height and depth.

Some opticians use an apparatus called an Intuitive Colorimeter to diagnose these problems and then to prescribe coloured overlays or tinted lenses (glasses). Also there are several Irlen Centres throughout Great Britain with trained practitioners who do likewise. The Irlen Centres train teachers and other adults as pre-screeners who after asking a range of questions and carrying out a series of activities can judge whether the pupil needs to use an overlay or a combination of overlays in order to read more efficiently.

After being given either overlays or the tinted glasses many individuals show a marked difference in the way they cope with the reading process. However, it has to be noted that overlays and glasses do not 'cure' reading problems. They take away any strain or visual 'anomalies' that might have previously been experienced.

ADD (Attention Deficit Disorder)

ADD is a form of brain dysfunction where there is chemical imbalance within the brain. This affects the child so that he or she finds it extremely difficult to concentrate and maintain attention. There is impulsivity of behaviour which leads the child to say or act without thinking first. The child also becomes hyperactive and finds it hard to listen to those in authority and act on what is said. Behaviour modification programmes are organised but also medication is prescribed. These help to control the behaviour so that the child is more able to learn.

It is often queried what is the difference between a child with behavioural problems and one with ADD. In brief one should look at where the unacceptable behaviours occur. If they are widespread within lessons and situations that are enjoyable and also within the home situation they are probably those pertaining to ADD and are not of the child's volition. If they occur only in certain lessons, such as the difficult ones of literacy and/or numeracy, then behaviour management plus some change within the learning-teaching situation should change the undesirable situation.

In some educational circles ADD (and its companion ADHD, Attention Deficit Hyperactivity Disorder) is part of the dyslexia 'stable'. Others recognise that any child might suffer from ADD.

Appendix 4
Information About the Language Areas

Receptive (understanding) language
The child may have problems with:

- following instructions and needs constant repetition;

- understanding jokes, language that is not literal (tends to be a literalist);

- understanding vocabulary;

- comprehension on reading assessments which scores at a weaker level than the scores on the accuracy reading level;

- listening skills which will be weak;

- poor understanding of time vocabulary;

- understanding (and giving) rhymes;

- phonological awareness (cannot understand the segmentation of words into syllables and/or phonemes).

Expressive (using) language
The child may have problems with:

- recalling words (uses descriptions etc. and use of time and position words);

- the use and misuse of pronouns, past tenses, plurals;

- articulation (plus the production of malapropisms);

- labelling;

- descriptive and imaginative language which is simply and poorly expressed;

- phonological awareness (cannot segment words into syllables and/or phonemes);

- sentence construction (either speaks with long confused sentences or only uses short phrases or one word answers);

- retelling events, stories or expanding what has been said.

Appendix 5
Simultaneous Oral Spelling Techniques (SOS)

This method of learning to spell is particularly useful for those children who have poor visual retentive memories and who need to learn commonly used words (irregular high frequency or keywords).

Before embarking on this method the teacher should make sure that the child is able to recognise and say all the names of the letters of the alphabet, both upper and lower case. It is also more beneficial if the child has learnt to write in a cursive script so that the hand flows through the letters.

Method

- The adult writes the word and says it.

- The child looks at it and repeats the word.

- The child spells the word out loud saying the letter names.

- The child copies the word (in a cursive script if possible), naming the letters as they are written.

- The child reads the written word.

- The child writes over the word saying the letter names.

- The child covers the word and writes it from memory, continuing to say the letters in their correct sequence.

- The child checks the written attempt with the original.

As well as writing and saying the word an extra step can be added where plastic or wooden letters are used to sequence the letters correctly before the child attempts the written version.

References and Further Reading

Alston, J. (1995) *Assessing and Promoting Writing Skills – New Edition.* Tamworth: NASEN.

Arnold, H. (1983) *Listening to Children Reading.* London: Hodder and Stoughton.

Augur, J. (undated) *Dyslexia – Early Help – Better Future.* Reading: The British Dyslexia Association.

Beveridge, S. (1996) *Learning Difficulties.* Tamworth: NASEN.

Bradley, L. (1984) *Assessing Reading Difficulties.* Windsor: NFER-Nelson.

Broomfield, H. & Combley, M. (1997) *Overcoming Dyslexia: a practical handbook for the classroom.* London: Whurr.

Chinn, S. & Ashcroft, J. (1998) *Mathematics for Dyslexics: A Teaching Handbook.* Second Edition. London: Whurr.

Clay, M. (1985) *The Early Detection of Reading Difficulties – Third Edition.* Auckland: Heinemann.

Connor, M. (1994) 'Specific learning difficulty (dyslexia) and interventions', *Support for Learning,* 9, 3, pp.114–119.

Cripps, C. & Peters, M. (1983) *Catchwords.* London: Harcourt Brace Jovanovich.

Crisfield, J. (1994) *The Dyslexia Handbook 1995.* The British Dyslexia Association: Reading (these handbooks are issued each year). Reading: BDA.

Crisfield, J. & Smythe, I. (1993) *The Dyslexia Handbook 1993/4.* Reading: The British Dyslexia Association.

Crombie, M. (1991) *Specific Learning Difficulties (Dyslexia) – A Teacher's Guide.* Glasgow: Jordanhill Sales and Publications.

DfEE (1994) *The Code of Practice on the Identification and Assessment of Special Educational Needs.* London: HMSO.

DfEE (1998) *The National Literacy Strategy*. London: HMSO.

DfEE (2000) *SEN Code of Practice on the Identification and Assessment of Pupils with Special Educational Needs and SEN Thresholds: Good Practice Guidance on Identification and Provision for Pupils with Special Educational Needs (draft code and guidance)*. Annesley: DfES.

DfES (2001) *SEN Toolkit*. Annesley: DfES.

DfES (2001) *Special Educational Needs Code of Practice*. Annesley: DfES.

Dyslexia – Your Questions Answered (undated) Reading: The British Dyslexia Association.

The Dyspraxia Trust (undated) *Praxis Makes Perfect*. Buckinghamshire: The Dyspraxis Trust.

El Naggar, O. (1996) *Specific Learning Difficulties in Mathematics: A Classroom Approach*. Tamworth: NASEN.

Helier, C. (1994) 'Closing the gap: Compensating for literacy delay in children with specific learning difficulties/dyslexia', *Support for Learning*, 9, 4, pp.162–165.

Holloway, J. (2000) *Dyslexia in Focus at Sixteen Plus: An Inclusive Teaching Approach*. Tamworth: NASEN.

Irlen, H. (1991) *Reading by the Colours*. New York: Avery Publishing Group.

Macintyre, C. (2000) *Dyspraxia 5 – 11*. London: Fulton.

Malone, G. & Smith, D. (1996) *Learning to Learn: Developing study skills with children who have special educational needs*. Tamworth: NASEN.

Ostler, C. (1991) *Dylsexia: A Parents' Survival Guide*. Godalming: Ammonite Books.

Ott, P. (1997) *How to Detect and Manage Dyslexia: A Reference and Resource Manual*. Oxford: Heinemann.

Peters, M. & Smith, B. (1993) *Spelling in Context*. Windsor: NFER-Nelson.

Pinsent, P. (Ed.) (1990) *Children with Literacy Difficulties*. London: Fulton.

Pollock, J. & Walker, E. (1994) *Day-to-Day Dyslexia in the Classroom*. London: Routledge.

Pumfrey, P. & Reason, R. (1991) *Specific Learning Difficulties (Dyslexia) – Challenges and Responses*. Windsor: NFER-Nelson.

QCA/DfEE (2000) *Curriculum Guidance for the Foundation Stage*. London: QCA/DfEE.

Reason, R. & Boote, R. (1994) *Learning Difficulties in Reading and Writing*. London: Routledge.

Reid, G. (1998) *Dyslexia: A Practitioner's Handbook*. Second Edition. Chichester: Wiley.

Smith, D. (Ed.) (2000) *Success in the Literacy Hour*. Tamworth: NASEN.

Smith, D. (2001) *Working with Children with Specific Learning Difficulties in the Early Years*. Lichfield: QEd.

Snowling, M. & Stackhouse, J. (Ed.) (1996) *Dyslexia, Speech and Language: A Practitioner's Handbook*. London: Whurr Publishers.

Tansley, P. & Pankhurst, J. (1981) *Children with Specific Learning Difficulties*. Windsor: NFER-Nelson.

Tod, J. (2000) *Individual Education Plans: Dyslexia*. London: Fulton.

Tyre, C. (1994) *Specific Learning Difficulties*. Lichfield: QEd Publications.

Warnock Report (1978) *Special Educational Needs*. London: HMSO.

Materials and Tests

Brand, V., *Spelling Made Easy*. Baldock: Egon Publishers Ltd.

Conner's Rating Scales: Revised. Windsor: NFER-Nelson.

Distar, McGraw-Hill-SRA.

Dunn et al., *British Picture Vocabulary Scale*. Windsor: NFER-Nelson.

Elliott, L., *S.T.R.A.N.D.S.*, Winchester SO23 8UG.

Fawcett, A. & Nicholson, R. (1995) *Dyslexia Early Screening Test (DEST)*. London: The Psychological Corporation.

Fawcett, A. & Nicholson, R. (1996) *Dyslexia Screening Test (DST)*. London: The Psychological Corporation.

Franklin Elementary Spellmaster (and other products), Reading: Electronic Learning Products.

Fuzzbuzz Reading Scheme. Oxford: Oxford University Press.

Graded Word Reading Test. Windsor: NFER-Nelson.

Hickey, K. (1992) *The Hickey Multisensory Language Course. Second edition*. London: Whurr Publishers.

Hornsby, B. & Shear, F. (1974) *Alpha to Omega*. Cambridge: LDA.

Moseley, D. & Nicol, C. (1989) *ACE Dictionary*. Cambridge: LDA.

Neale, M., *Analysis of Reading Ability*. Second Edition. Windsor: NFER-Nelson.

North, C. & Parker, M. (1993) *Phonological Awareness Pack*. Summerhill, Althorne CM3 6BY.

Raven, J., *Progressive Marices and Vocabulary Scales*. Windsor: NFER-Nelson.

Richards, J. (1988) *Attack Your Reading, Writing, Spelling Problems – Our Way*.

Salford Sentence Reading Test. London: Hodder and Stoughton.

Schedule of Growing Skills: Second Edition. Windsor: NFER-Nelson.

Singleton, C. (1996) *Keystage 1 CoPS*, Chameleon Educational Systems Ltd., Southwell.

Stone et al., *Beat Dyslexia*. Wisbech: LDA.

THRASS, Collins Educational.

Vincent, D. & de la Mare, M., *Individual Reading Analysis*. Windsor: NFER-Nelson.

Vincent, D. & de la Mare, M., *New Reading Analysis*. Windsor: NFER-Nelson.

Wendon, L. (1987) *Letterland Teaching Programmes 1 & 2*. Cambridge: Letterland Ltd.

Young, D. (1983) *Parallel Spelling Tests*. London: Hodder and Stoughton.

Useful Addresses

The British Dyslexia Association, 98 London Road, Reading RG1 5AU.

The Dyslexia Institute, 133 Gresham Road, Staines, Middlesex TW18 2AJ.

The Dyspraxia Foundation, 8 West Alley, Hitchin, Herts. SG5 1EG.

Helen Arkell Dyslexia Centre, Frensham, Farnham, Surrey GU10 3BW.

Irlen Centres (see local telephone directories for the nearest regional centre).

NFER-Nelson, Unit 28, Bramble Road, Techno Trading Centre, Swindon, Wiltshire SN2 8EZ.

Taskmaster Resources, Taskmaster Ltd., Morris Road, Leicester LE2 6BR.